PRAISE FOR
*I AM NOT AFRAID: DEMON POSSESSION
AND SPIRITUAL WARFARE*

This timely publication introduces the joyous salvation that Christ's mission brings to nations globally in His stead, by His command and promise, who conquered sin, death, and devil victoriously and vicariously. Dr. Bennett opens up fascinating insights into foreign realms of Madagascar and its flourishing Lutheran Church, reaching across barriers of disbelief, paganism, idolatry—liberating from the clutches of evil. He demonstrates how this merciful deliverance was part of Christ's Gospel and the Church's mission from the start. May this receive all the attention it deserves and invite many to study the exiting world of faithful missions in Africa!

—Bishop Dr. Wilhelm Weber
Lutheran Church in Southern Africa

This is truly a remarkable book. Written with genuine pastoral concern by a minister of the LCMS, it first introduces the reader to the practice of exorcism in the Malagasy Lutheran Church based on the author's original field research before surveying relevant biblical episodes and Lutheran teachings on demonic possession and exorcism. Based on well-documented doctrinal reassurance, Bennett encourages pastors and others to learn from the African sister church how to make people experience the "joy from deliverance of bondage." Everyone engaged in pastoral ministry will greatly benefit from studying this book.

—Christoffer H. Grundmann
John R. Eckrich University Chair in Religion and the Healing Arts
Valparaiso University
Author of *Sent to heal!* (2005).

Although thoroughly Lutheran, this timely work will be of interest not just to Lutherans and to those who share all its perspectives. It will be of interest to readers interested in the global church, in current views about demonology, and in Reformation views and especially historic Lutheran views about demonology. I found this book too fascinating to put down, especially in the interviews section; the field observations offer a distinctive contribution.

—Craig S. Keener, MDiv, PhD
Professor of New Testament
Asbury Theological Seminary

The activity of the devil and his demons is readily denied by many Christians in the United States and Europe. Therefore, I find it amazing to finally find a book in the English language that correctly understands and faithfully depicts the Malagasy Lutheran Church, particularly the department of the *Fifohazana*. Through his research, Dr. Bennett has provided an opportunity for English readers to gain an understanding of Malagasy context and reality. This book demonstrates the scriptural basis of the *Fifohazana* movement's theology and practice.

Dr. Bennett is one of the few scholars who have shown interest in this area as a researcher. He opens a window for continued research into an area of theology that has been long lost to Western Christianity. Dr. Bennett's discovery of Confessional Lutheranism as found in the Malagasy Lutheran Church provides others with an opportunity to understand how Confessional Lutheranism can deal with the spiritual problems of this age.

This book is also helpful for the Lutheran Church of Madagascar as it continues to catechize its members and to battle the ongoing influences of syncretism and postmodernism found in liberal theology.

—Rev. Dr. David Rakotonirina
Bishop of Antananarivo
Madagascar

Dr. Bennett writes about an important aspect that has been almost forgotten in our spiritual understanding and practice of God's Word. Describing the Malagasy Lutheran context, Dr. Bennett, in this outstanding book, helps us to look at Scripture and Lutheran theology in our postmodern context and rediscover a spiritual struggle that directs our ministry to the ultimate authority of Jesus over Satan and his allies. The Western Church can once again examine exorcism, demon possession, and spiritual warfare, and in an evangelistic context practice the Christian faith with the power of the Holy Spirit.

—Reverend Professor Clóvis Jair Prunzel
Concordia Seminary and ULBRA, Brasil

Upon reading Dr. Bennett's book, we are reminded that there are angels among us—both the holy and the evil. In his study of the Lutherans in Madagascar, Dr. Bennett shows that these Christians must deal with the devil and his angels directly as did our Lord and the apostles. The Malagasy Lutherans, perhaps more than their western brothers and sisters, understand God's Word and Sacraments to be the means by which our Lord works through His Church to release people from demonic control, bring them into Christ, and Satan's kingdom of darkness is pushed pack and held at bay.

Dr. Bennett's Book, *I Am Not Afraid: Demon Possession and Spiritual Warfare*, is a gift to the Church, for in it is presented a view of spiritual warfare and exorcism that is grounded in the Scriptures and connected to the life and work of the Church—a much needed perspective for the modern Christian.

—Rev. Thomas W. Dunseth
Associate Director of Deaf Mission for Asia, Lutheran Friends of the Deaf/Mill Neck Family of Organizations
Missionary pastor for the Deaf in the Michigan District, LCMS

I Am Not Afraid: Demon Possession and Spiritual Warfare

I AM NOT AFRAID: DEMON POSSESSION AND SPIRITUAL WARFARE

TRUE ACCOUNTS FROM THE LUTHERAN CHURCH OF MADAGASCAR

ROBERT H. BENNETT

Peer Reviewed

CONCORDIA PUBLISHING HOUSE · SAINT LOUIS

A free downloadable Study Guide for *I Am Not Afraid: Demon Possession and Spiritual Warfare* is available on cph.org.

Peer Reviewed

Published 2013 by Concordia Publishing House
3558 S. Jefferson Ave., St. Louis, MO 63118–3968
1-800-325-3040 • www.cph.org

Library of Congress Cataloging-in-Publication Data

Bennett, Robert H.

I am not afraid : demon possession and spiritual warfare : true accounts from the Lutheran Church of Madagascar / Robert H. Bennett.

pages cm.

Includes bibliographical references and index.

ISBN 978-0-7586-4198-4

1. Fiangonana Loterana Malagasy. 2. Spiritual warfare—Madagascar. 3. Demonology—Madagascar. 4. Demoniac possession—Madagascar. I. Title.

BX8063.M28B46 2013

235'.409691--dc23   2013002988

5 6 7 8 9 10   22 21 20 19 18 17 16

CONTENTS

LIST OF ILLUSTRATIONS

FOREWORD

Talk of exorcism, demonic possession, and spiritual warfare is likely to evoke some suspicion among Christians from North America and Europe. Even though these realities are spoken of in the Holy Scriptures and attested to the history of the Church catholic, they are apt to be dismissed or explained away by Christians living under subtle influences of Enlightenment skepticism. Such was not the case for Martin Luther, who knew that "sin, death and the Devil were not a theological problem to be solved—they were enemies to be fought against. The problem of evil is not primarily a problem within the sphere of the intellect, and it would be foolish to try to solve it there. The true fight is not carried out with syllogisms, but with prayer and preaching."[1] Luther's spiritual offspring in the Malagasy Lutheran Church resonate with the Reformer's profound understanding of the old evil foe's attacks on body and soul, in his effort to unseat Christ Jesus. Malagasy Lutherans can teach us how to pray the Seventh Petition of the Lord's Prayer, "Deliver us from evil," with an awareness that we are praying against the Adversary as we call upon our Father to rescue us from every evil.

Having been to Madagascar several times in the last few years both with seminarians on study trips and as a guest lecturer, I have seen much of what Robert Bennett writes about in *I Am Not Afraid: Demon Possession and Spiritual Warfare.* Norwegian Lutheran missionaries came to Madagascar in 1866. The legacy of their dedicated and often painful labor is a large and growing Lutheran Church that is maintained by a confessional, conservative Lutheran theology and is marked by a vibrant life of mercy and outreach. One of the elements distinctive of the Malagasy Lutherans is the practice of exorcism in evangelization and spiritual care. Robert Bennett, who has made numerous trips to Madagascar to do field research for this book, examines the phenomena of demonic activity along with the

---

[1] Esko Murto, "An Iron Wall on Our Side: Martin Luther's Understanding of the Christian Devotional Life as a Battleground Against the Devil" in *Theology is Eminently Practical: Essays in Honor of John T. Pless*, edited by Jacob Corzine and Bryan Wolfmueller (Fort Wayne: Lutheran Legacy Press, 2012), 130.

practice of exorcism in the Malagasy context. For this reason alone his book represents a major contribution to missiological research giving us a glimpse into the revival movement (*fifohazana*), life in the *toby* (encampments of mercy operated by the church to provide holistic care), and the extraordinary work of the *mpiandry* (lay people trained and commissioned by the church) who serve to evangelize, show mercy, and guide converts to the pastor for catechetical instruction and Baptism.

Yet there is much more to Bennett's work that will benefit not only missionaries but also theologians and pastors. North American pastors are also confronted with circumstances that give evidence of demonic activity and are often uncertain how to respond. *Lutheran Service Book: Pastoral Care Companion* (St. Louis: Concordia, 2007) contains a section of resources under the heading "Occult Practices and Demonic Affliction" providing pastoral guidance, biblical readings, Psalms, hymn stanzas, and prayers for pastors to use in situations such as these. These resources were not available in previous agendas and pastoral companions of The Lutheran Church— Missouri Synod or other North American Lutheran bodies. Bennett's biblical and theological treatment of the demonic will assist pastors seeking to minister to people who experience satanic attack. *I Am Not Afraid: Demon Possession and Spiritual Warfare* fills a void in Lutheran pastoral theology; it will be practically helpful to pastors confronting this dark albeit often disguised spiritual condition in our culture.

The magisterial, two volume work, *Miracles: The Credibility of the New Testament Accounts* by New Testament scholar Craig Keener links Jesus' exorcism of demons and unclean spirits with what Bennett and others have observed in Madagascar.[2] Keener also provides strong arguments to counter the skepticism of both those who would dent the veracity of the New Testament accounts as well as their counterparts in places like Madagascar. *I Am Not Afraid: Demon Possession and Spiritual Warfare* rightly deserves a place alongside of Keener's exegetical treatment as a particular Lutheran contribution. Dr. Bennett, who is also a parish pastor, has provided readers with an engaging and carefully documented study that will

---

[2] Craig Keener, *Miracles: The Credibility of the New Testament Accounts* (Grand Rapids: Baker Academic Press, 2011), 1:315.

help western readers learn some valuable lessons from our Malagasy brothers and sisters. Indeed, we do have much to learn and we should be grateful to Dr. Bennett for giving us a readable and interesting introduction.

John T. Pless
Assistant Professor of Pastoral Theology and Missions
Concordia Theological Seminary
Fort Wayne, Indiana
Ash Wednesday, 2013

ACKNOWLEDGEMENTS

I would like to thank and acknowledge the many people of Madagascar who have patiently endured hours of my questioning and who have welcomed me into their homes and churches during the time of my field research. This book was only possible because of the tremendous love and openness extended to me. Without their openness and willingness, it would have been extremely difficult to collect the data necessary for this research.

I would especially like to single out the Rev. Dr. Joseph Randrianasolo. Dr. Randrianasolo not only provided the aid of his graduate class of the SALT Seminary as interviewers to collect the numerous data contained within this dissertation, but also acted as field director, translator, and informal advisor throughout the entire process of this research. He has become a dear friend and valued consultant providing reliable guidance throughout the research process while at the same time ensuring that the Malagasy Lutheran Church is properly represented within this book.

I also want to thank my wife, Angela, and children, Robert, Joseph, Amy, and Kate without whose support this book could not have begun to be accomplished. In addition, I must thank my advisor, Rev. Dr. Detlev Schulz and his wife Cornelia for providing fellowship and lodging opportunities as I traveled between my home in Michigan and my residential requirements at Concordia Theological Seminary, Fort Wayne, IN. In addition to her incredible hospitality, Cornelia has also tirelessly devoted her time by providing editorial assistance throughout the writing process.

Finally, I give thanks and praise to my Lord Jesus Christ who has faithfully worked through the numerous individuals that have delivered the Holy Word and the Holy Sacraments to me, thereby connecting to the forgiveness provided though His life, death, and resurrection. The most noteworthy of these being the sainted Rev. Dr. Ralph Fisher who not only continually spoke the Gospel into my young ears, but also instilled within me a strong desire for higher learning. To God be the praise.

ABBREVIATIONS

AIC   African Independent Church

FJKM   Fiangonan'i Jesoa Kristy Eto Madagasikara—Church of Jesus Christ in Madagascar

FLM   Fiangonana Loterana Malagasy—Malagasy Lutheran Church

LMS   London Missionary Society

LWF   Lutheran World Federation

NMS   Norwegian Mission Society

SALT   *Sekoly Ambony Loterana momba ny Teolojia* (Malagasy Lutheran Graduate Seminary located in Fianarantsoa)

KEY TERMS

ambirorandrano. A spiritual being that resembles a mystical mermaid. May also be called *Zazavavindrano* or *Zazavavirano.*

angabe. Great ghost or the oldest ghost.

angatra. A ghost.

Antakarana. Name of the region and consequently of a tribe, who lives in the region of Antsiranana or former Diego Suarez.

betsimisaraka. It is one of the eighteen tribes of Madagascar. They live on the east coast in the region of Toamasina or former Tamatave.

bilo. A possessing entity (many time of a snake or animal spirit) originating within the Antandroy and Bara tribes.

dady. Royal relics of the kings.

doany. Royal ancestral spirits.

famadihana. A ceremony that consists of removing the remains of ancestors from the family tomb and wrapping them in new shrouds.

fanahy ratsy. Evil spirit.

fifohazana. Term used for the revival movement in Madagascar.

fitampoha. Royal bath, bathing of the royal relics.

helo. Spirits that are known for possessing people without their invitation.

kasoa. A spiritual possession that appears as madness connected to love affairs.

lamba mena. A decorative cloth for wrapping the body.

lolo. Name of a nature spirit; literally: butterfly.

maha-lonaky. What makes one old and wise man. In some cases, it is linked to an active role in traditional religion.

Malagasy. Refers to the inhabitants of the island of Madagascar.

matoatoa. A ghost.

moasy. Herbalist-healers. May be used as a synonym for *ombiasy*.

mpiandry. Shepherd; special trained laity within the Fifohazana who commits their lives to live as servants to Jesus.

nenilava. Tall mother; the name given to revival leader Volahavana Germaine who is specifically attached to the Ankarmalaza *toby*.

njarinintsy. A ghost. The literal meaning is that which "makes you cold" (opposite of warm), or can mean, "that which frightens."

ombiasy. Healer, seer, advisor, spirit medium, shaman.

razana. The collective body of ancestral spirits.

sikidy. Divination system written in Arabic script dating back to pre-colonial Malagasy history.

toby. Revival center, camp, place of healing that provides for the sick whereas clergy and doctors work together in a holistic way to care for the people.

tromba. Ancestral spirit; spirit possession ceremony.

vazimba. Original inhabitant, spirit of original inhabitants.

mivoaka. Depart; go out.

zanahary. The name of the creator god.

Zazavavindrano. See *ambirorandrano*.

PART ONE

THE MALAGASY STORY

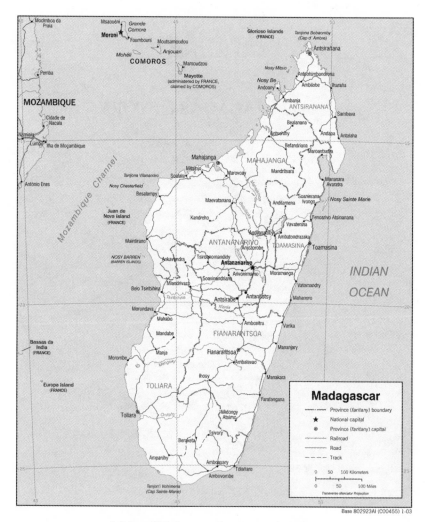

1. Map of Madagascar from www.cia.gov.

CHAPTER ONE

DEPART YOU EVIL SPIRITS

*He uncovers the deeps out of darkness and brings deep
darkness to light.*

—Job 12:22

In August 2007, I visited Toliara, a town off the coast of western
Madagascar. My purpose was to attend a five-day worship event
sponsored by the *Fifohazana* movement of the Malagasy Lutheran
Church. At the conclusion of each day's events, the participants, who
numbered in the thousands, would line up in rows while others would
stand between them dressed in white gowns. After a few hymns,
Bible readings, and a short expository sermon, the people began to
speak in unison, "Depart you evil spirits in the name of Jesus." What I
had ventured into was a mass exorcism. I immediately noticed that
this exorcism was not focused on any specific individuals, but upon
the place itself and the general assembly. Later, I learned that the
exorcism was meant to cast out any evil that may have been residing
in the area of the general assembly and to identify anyone who may
be possessed or stricken by an evil spirit. Thousands of people were
sitting upon the dirty ground watching the ritual. One woman, who sat
outside the group observing the commotion, began to change her
demeanor. She began screaming and making wailing sounds. Those
speaking the exorcistic words moved to her location and began
speaking directly to her, "Depart you evil spirits in the name of
Jesus." She flung her body up and down upon the ground, but those
present restrained her and continued to call upon the name of Jesus.
As time went on her reactions grew in intensity until finally she began
to pray in the name of Jesus. At that time, everything seemed to quiet

and return to normal. A spirit had possessed her. Similar events occurred in the crowd over the coming days. What was going on in the minds of those who experienced possession? This book answers this question by thoroughly examining the phenomena of exorcism found in the Lutheran Church of Madagascar (FLM). The focus of this book is from a Lutheran Christian perspective; however, the data provided crosses over denominational lines making it accessible to anyone seeking to learn more about the topic of exorcism. While some may conclude that this topic is out-of-date or fanciful, there are many who are searching for direction in the area of exorcism. This book is an excellent resource, especially in a time when the Western world seems to be reverting to paganism.

BEGINNINGS

My interest in the Malagasy Lutheran Church began in 2006 when I met Dr. Joseph Randrianasolo, who would quickly become one of my best friends and mentors. Dr. Randrianasolo grew up in a syncretistic Roman Catholic home in Madagascar. His family attended church, and they also participated in the traditional religions of the Malagasy people (animism.) At age twelve, Randrianasolo, at the request of his family, entered a Roman Catholic seminary to begin training for the priesthood. When Randrianasolo reached adulthood, he was ordained. While performing his duties as a priest, he began to notice the work of a Lutheran movement called the *Fifohazana*. While attending one of their gatherings he observed an exorcism. What happened next came unexpectedly: he lost consciousness and fell to the ground. Those present saw him in convulsions and recognized that he was under attack by demonic forces. The *mpiandry* (laymen who work with the ordained clergy) ran to his side and began to focus their exorcistic words on him. After regaining consciousness, he vowed to leave both the Roman Catholic priesthood and the traditional religions of his family to become a Lutheran pastor. He would also study the ways of the *mpiandry,* eventually becoming one of its leaders. This began his thirty-plus year career as a Lutheran pastor, seminary professor, and exorcist. It is only through the friendship of this man that I was able to write this book. His leadership within the movement allowed me to obtain an insider's perspective of the *Fifohazana* movement (revival movement) and access to hundreds of converts who had entered the Christian Church through the exorcistic rituals of

4

the Malagasy Lutheran Church. This book is about them, the trials they faced before coming to the Christian faith, and their new lives of freedom lived in the church.

Part one of this book focuses specifically on the spiritual warfare found within the Malagasy Lutheran Church. Included in this section are recent conversations dealing with spiritual warfare, an introduction into the Malagasy Lutheran Church, and the traditional Malagasy worldview. These are the stories of those who have been rescued from the darkness of sin and brought into the light of the Gospel.

Part two of the book looks to the Bible and the Church for explanation and historical perspective on the spiritual warfare found in the Malagasy Lutheran Church. Is spiritual warfare something new to the Church? Is it something only found in the time of Jesus and the apostles? What has the Church said in the past about such activities? Part two of the book examines many of these questions by reviewing the New Testament's spiritual warfare themes, exploring the views of Martin Luther and other Lutheran leaders, and finally providing some helpful contemporary material and resources for dealing with spiritual warfare in today's context.

WHAT'S SO SPECIAL
ABOUT THE LUTHERAN CHURCH OF MADAGASCAR?

The Christian Church continues to see considerable growth on the island of Madagascar. The total population of this island is not overwhelming (approximately 21 million).[1] However, the rate of Christian conversion requires any student of Christianity to take notice. While just over half of the island's population (52%) follows the traditional religion of animism, the Christian Church (41%) continues to increase in size and influence within the culture. The Lutheran Church of Madagascar has experienced an increase of approximately three million members just over the past decade.[2] The

---

[1] "CIA - The World Factbook," Welcome to the CIA Web Site—Central Intelligence Agency, People, https://www.cia.gov/library/publications/the-world-factbook/geos/ma.html (accessed August 09, 2010).

[2] This number is an estimate. Because of the remoteness of the Island and the lack or reporting procedures found within the FLM no reliable number is available at the time of this writing.

majority of this growth is conversion growth from the animistic population. Many believe that *mpiandry* movement is the most influential factor in the growth of the Malagasy Lutheran Church.[3]

The term *mpiandry* is associated with the *Fifohazana* movement or revival.[4] This movement has dispatched thousands of trained evangelists into the countryside who are prepared to deal with the daily problems of the population, such as sickness, poverty, and spiritual matters. They not only evangelize the native peoples, but also minister to them daily, through their interactions and prayers. Hymns, Bible study, and preaching are integral to the daily lives of the people.

The universal Church can benefit by learning from the Malagasy Lutheran Church about the realities of the existence of Satan, his activities, and Jesus' victory over him.[5] The western world is in transition with paganism on the rise. Spiritualism is progressively becoming a dominant religious preference within a postmodern age.[6] The Malagasy Lutherans have adapted their approach to reach the animistic population by relying upon the Holy Scriptures as the foundation of their approach. They have addressed the problem of mingling traditional religions with the purity of the Gospel (syncretism) head-on in a society, which at its roots inherited such practices from its earliest recorded history.[7] The Malagasy Lutherans have at the same time refused to accept the enlightenments denial of spiritual forces, which interact with humanity. The *mpiandry* movement mobilizes their members to go out and tell the good news

---

[3] Joseph Randrianasolo, "Spirits in Madagascar," interview by author, August 3, 2009.

[4] "The term *revival* tends to bring with it a lot of baggage in the American context. Such a term carries with it the baggage of the highly charged emotional revivals of early American history. This 'baggage' should not influence our understanding of what is occurring in Madagascar. The revival that is taking place in the Malagasy Lutheran Church is very objective in nature centered on an orderly proclamation of Holy Scripture."

[5] See Christopher H. Rosik, "When Discernment Fails: The Case for Outcome Studies on Exorcism," *Journal of Psychology and Theology* 25, no. 3 (1997): 354.

[6] "Spiritual Survey: New Study Points to Rise of Do-It-Yourself Religion," The Wall of Separation, Pew Forum, http://blog.au.org/2009/12/10/spiritual-survey-new-study-points-to-rise-of-doityourself-religion/ (accessed February 28, 2010).

[7] See Bakoly Domenichini-Ramiaramanana, "The Church and Malagasy Culture," *Exchange* 22, no. 1 (1993): 47.

of the Gospel in a way that answers the questions of their society—
questions such as spirit possession and the power of the ancestors.[8] If
the western world is reverting to an animistic worldview, the Western
Church could do well to learn from the Malagasy Lutherans.

RECENT CONVERSATIONS AND LITERATURE

It is hard to avoid the staggering growth of the Malagasy Lutheran
Church and other African Independent Churches (AIC). There has
only been minimal literature produced describing the *mpiandry*
movement of the Malagasy Lutheran Church, especially if one
restricts the search to the English language. However, within recent
years, this trend has begun to change. Two of the in-depth works
produced are *The Fifohazana,* edited by Cynthia Holder-Rich, and
Shepherds and Demons, a doctoral dissertation, now a book by Hans
Austnaberg. Each is laden with information and research not
previously available to the western world. Holder's book contains a
series of essays that describe the basis and history of the *Fifohazana*
movement. Austnaberg narrows his research to the topic of exorcism
in the movement.[9] Both of these books are helpful; however, they
lack an insider's perspective. Austnaberg claims to have
accomplished this perspective, but his research is demonstrative,
rather than representing individual narratives.[10] Rather than following
Austnaberg's and Holder-Rich's methodology we will capture the
lived experience of the people through a series of interviews, which
describe how the members of the *mpiandry* view the events
surrounding their own conversion experiences and how exorcism is
used as one of the primary tools of the Church. The graduate students
of the SALT Seminary in Fianarantsoa have graciously conducted
many of the interviews that make up this book.[11] Dr. Randrianasolo

---

[8] The *mpiandry* acts in conjunction with the *Fifohazana* movement, which is a
recognized department of the Malagasy Lutheran Church.

[9] Hans Austnaberg, *Shepherds and Demons: A Study of Exorcism As Practiced and
Understood by Shepherds in the Malagasy Lutheran Church* (New York: Peter Lang,
2007), 15.

[10] Austnaberg, *Shepherds and Demons*, 15.

[11] This was the first Lutheran Seminary to be established in the Malagasy Lutheran
Church. It is still located in Fianarantsoa, a large city found in the southeastern
portion of the island. The students of this seminary are seeking graduate level

translated all the interviews to insure continuity. Four main areas make up the structure of the interviews. The first question seeks an understanding of the respondents' worldviews prior to their conversions. The second seeks to answer how those interviewed became associated with the Malagasy Lutheran Church. The third question gets to the heart of this book, that is, how the people understand their conversion experience and what, if any, function exorcism played in that conversion. Finally, the fourth question provides a glimpse into the cultic lives of the converts now that they are members of the Malagasy Lutheran Church. These questions are the focus of part one of this book and bring an insider's perspective of those who have experienced demonic oppression, possession, and exorcism, and have been set free through the means of the Word of God. Jesus has said, "Come to Me, all who labor and are heavy laden, and I will give you rest" (Matthew 11:28–30). Through the gift exorcism, Jesus continues to provide rest to a people caught in the deep darkness of demonic possession. It is my hope that this book brings peace and rest to many who are searching for answers to questions of demonic oppression and possession.

2. The SALT Graduate Seminary in *Fianarantsoa* Madagascar.

---

degrees, all of whom have already completed undergraduate degrees at one of the denomination's six regional seminaries located on the island.

CHAPTER TWO

DRAMATIC CONVERSIONS

MAKING SENSE OF POPULAR
SPIRITUAL WARFARE THEMES

For we do not wrestle against flesh and blood, but against the rulers, against the authorities, against the cosmic powers over this present darkness, against the spiritual forces of evil in the heavenly places.

—Ephesians 6:12

If you go to any bookstore these days you will find dozens of books referring to spiritual warfare, demonic activity, and exorcism. Hollywood continues to release movies on the subject, and popular news programs run stories that represent an upswing in such interests. Most of these books, movies, and television programs remain lost in the things of fantasy. This chapter will present some of the helpful books and authors on the subject while keeping the conversation historically and biblically based.

POWER EVANGELISM

The terms "power evangelism" and "power encounters" are foreign to many Christian vocabularies. Power evangelism is a term introduced by the John Wimber, Pentecostal preacher and former pastor of the Vineyard Christian Fellowship of Anaheim, California. Wimber introduced this term in one of his early books, which carried the same title, *Power Evangelism*. Early in his book, Wimber defines the word *power* in view of the kingdom of God.[1] Wimber suggests that when one becomes a Christian, one enters into a spiritual battle with Satan.[2] Moreover, Wimber understands Christians to be instruments of the kingdom, who have the responsibility to be witnesses to the power of Jesus.[3] He believes God works through individual Christians to fulfill His will. Wimber describes a "power encounter" as an encounter between man, Satan, and God.[4] He defines a "power encounter" as a demonstration of Jesus' power over all false gods and spirits that men seek to worship.[5] For Wimber, "power encounters" include exorcisms and healings.

David Burnett describes power encounters in more detail in his book titled, *Unearthly Powers: a Christian's Handbook on Primal and Folk Religions.* Burnett finds power encounters to be the activity that frees those lost in satanic darkness. For Burnett, demons are cast out, not through the means of a ritual, but instead through the action of Jesus. He understands the final goal of a power encounter to be freedom from idols and false worship.[6] However, unlike Burnett, Wimber does not find a power encounter as the final goal, but only a necessary step along the way. Conversion, for Wimber, requires something else—the power encounter must accompany what he calls "power evangelism." Wimber means the presentation of the Gospel, namely, the work of Jesus upon the cross and His resurrection from the grave. Wimber is clear; a miracle or sign cannot rescue the sinner from damnation. Only the substitutionary work of Jesus can bring life to the spiritually dead.[7]

For Wimber, power evangelism is not something found within men. Nor is it something that man can manipulate or control. To suggest such would be to embrace a magical understanding, such as animism. At the same time, Wimber maintains the necessity of divine

---

[1] John Wimber and Kevin Springer, *Power Evangelism* (London: Holder Christian Paperbacks, 2001), 28.

[2] Wimber and Springer, *Power Evangelism*, 38.

[3] Wimber and Springer, *Power Evangelism*, 43.

[4] Wimber and Springer, *Power Evangelism*, 52.

[5] Wimber and Springer, *Power Evangelism*, 53.

[6] David Burnett, *Unearthly Powers: a Christian's Handbook on Primal and Folk Religions* (Nashville: Oliver Nelson, 1992), 252.

[7] Wimber and Springer, *Power Evangelism*, 15.

power as an important part of the equation, especially to tribal people who worship in traditional ways. Wimber understands people to be in bondage to sin and evil. Therefore, power is necessary to free them. He finds the power of God a necessity to break through the resistance that all people have toward the Gospel.[8] Yet, according to his critics, Wimber adds to the Gospel a supposed power that is outside of the modern-day worldview. Wimber denies such claims and insists that he is only speaking in-line with the Bible.[9] Wimber suggests that many in the modern world have missed this essential aspect of evangelism. While Wimber's idea of power evangelism may be questionable by many, his point properly describes the situation in Madagascar when the first western missionaries arrived. They were preaching the Gospel, and as a result, conversions were occurring. However, with the conversions, many strange signs were happening. People were screaming out as they fell upon the ground and convulsed at the preaching of the Gospel. Faced with this strange behavior, the missionaries were at a loss as to how to respond. The *Fifohazana* movement filled this void.

Paul Hiebert, a well-known missiologist and author, shares Wimber's concern. Hiebert offers some additional warnings concerning the complications of power encounters. One warning is the possibility of becoming too reliant upon demonstrations of power rather than the Word of God. Hiebert finds such a reliance on power to result in ritualistic magic, rather than reliance on the grace of God and the authority of Jesus.[10] Hiebert's point is a reasonable starting point; however, the fact remains power encounters and power evangelism continue to be a significant occurrence in the clash that occurs between the Gospel and the traditional religions of Africa. The leaders of the Lutheran Church of Madagascar share Hiebert's caution concerning the term "power evangelism." Randrianasolo warns:

> Pentecostal doctrines tend to stress more on the Holy Spirit while still talking about Jesus Christ and more on miracles or extraordinary happenings than true conversions of the heart. Therefore, from that perspective, power evangelism may just

---

[8] Wimber and Springer, *Power Evangelism*, 78–79.

[9] Wimber and Springer, *Power Evangelism*, 79.

[10] Paul G. Hiebert, "Spiritual Warfare and Worldviews," *Direction* 29, no. 2 (2000): 123.

point to the healing of the body and to the departure of the evil spirits and may miss the point of lasting conversions to faith in Jesus Christ. Where are the place of repentance and justification by faith baptism? In exorcism, the real question is: So after being exorcised, what's next? The question is right because we talk about evangelism.[11]

In his book titled, *Mission from the Cross: The Lutheran Theology of Mission,* Dr. Klaus Detlev Schulz adds additional warnings that must be considered when speaking about power evangelism. He writes:

> It is true that in the conversion process the saving work of the Holy Spirit takes hold of a man's entire existence, thus his thinking, feelings, and desires. When God comes to a man, the Holy Spirit can also seize the heart as the innermost seat of man's spirituality (Rom. 8:16; Gal. 4:6) and instill very explicit emotions such as joy and peace (Rom. 15:13). Experiences of being gripped by God may accompany the saving work of the Holy Spirit (Rom. 14:17), such as, for example, speaking in tongues (1 Corinthians 14) or visions. But the latter experiences must be tested and interpreted against God's Word.[12]

Therefore, while not accepting Wimber's Pentecostal leaning doctrines, his phrase "power evangelism" and his definition of the before mentioned term is helpful in describing the reports of both the Malagasy Lutherans and many other church bodies in Africa and other parts of the world.[13] Moreover, there is much we can learn from

---

[11] Joseph Randrianasolo, "Some Reflections about the Dissertation Proposal Written by the Rev. Robert H. Bennett," e-mail message to author, February 14, 2010.

[12] Klaus Detlev Schulz, *Mission from the Cross: The Lutheran Theology of Mission* (St. Louis: Concordia, 2009), 138.

[13] Over the years, many additions have been made to Wimber's notion of power evangelism. These include something called "Strategic Level Spiritual Warfare." Such theology accepts the existence of "territorial spirits" and "spirit mapping" along with a host of other problematic concepts. See Samuel Hio-Kee Ooi, "A Study of Strategic Level Spiritual Warfare from a Chinese Perspective," *Asian Journal of Pentecostal Studies*, 9, no. 1 (2006): 143–161. Wimber's terminology is used in this book only within his original context.

the writings of these men that could be used in a western mission context.

SPIRITUAL WARFARE

"Spiritual warfare" is a technical term that describes the battle between God and Satan for the souls of people.[14] Many consider David Powlison to be one of the most prolific writers on the topic of spiritual warfare. In his book *Power Encounters: Reclaiming Spiritual Warfare*, Powlison acknowledges that all people are involved in a form of spiritual warfare. He goes so far as to identify all of history as a time of spiritual warfare—beginning in the Book of Genesis with the fall of man and concluding in the Book of Revelation with the triumph of Jesus.[15] Sin places people in the midst of this warfare. Powlison acknowledges that modern man is spiritually dead and no longer recognizes the war that is continuing in his midst. He identifies the problem of disbelief with the transformation of popular allegiances from biblical realities to the realities of chemistry, biology, neurology, psychology, and sociology, which have emptied scripture of its power.[16]

Powlison speaks the truth; humanity is in a precarious situation from which only the Lord Jesus can rescue. How can one survive a war if one does not recognize that the war is raging in one's midst? One who denies such things also tends to deny the reality of God's presence. In the midst of such a demythologizing theology, Powlison correctly concludes that prayer and worship become empty rituals that have no real effect and sin becomes simply social maladjustment.[17]

Powlison's warning is nothing new. The early missionary efforts in Madagascar tried to demythologize the people's understanding of demons, ancestors, and other spirits. At the same time, the missionaries were in actuality demythologizing the Scriptures. That is they were removing the spiritual realities from Scripture and replacing them with fanciful myths and diagnosis of psychological

---

[14] Schulz, *Mission from the Cross*, 138.

[15] David A. Powlison, *Power Encounters Reclaiming Spiritual Warfare* (Hourglass Books) (New York: Baker Books, 1995), 20–21.

[16] Powlison, *Power Encounters*, 23.

[17] Powlison, *Power Encounters*, 24.

diagnosis.[18] Such tactics left many without protection against spiritual attacks. The missionaries would not assist the demon possessed, but instead, thought them to be insane and in need of only medical or psychological healing. May the Lord protect us in the Church today from such disbelief and grant us eyes to see the spiritual battle that confronts us through the eyes of Him who has defeated sin, death, and the devil. "For we do not wrestle against flesh and blood, but against the rulers, against the authorities, against the cosmic powers over this present darkness, against the spiritual forces of evil in the heavenly places" (Ephesians 6:12).

---

[18] "Demythologization (Ger. *Entmythologisierung*)—Term used by R. Bultmann for a way of interpreting Scripture in the categories of modern man. It tries to remove ancient 'myths' (e.g., the 'mythical *Weltbild*') and state the message of Scripture in relevant contemporary language. He defined 'myth' as a representation according to which the transcendent and divine appears as immanent and human, the invisible as visible. The issue was discussed in 1941 by Bultmann in a study entitled *Offenbarung und Heilsgeschehen*. He believes that hidden in the *myth* is a *kerygma*, which can be set free by demythologization and proclaimed in existential terms . . . The hist. core of Christianity is in the crucifixion of Jesus, which is also in a mythological setting. Fritz Buri (b. 1907; Swiss theol.; prof. Basel) endorses Bultmann's existentialism and demythologization, but faults him for halting with the *kerygma*. Consistency, he holds, requires also a 'dekerygmatization' of the Christian message." Erwin L. Lueker, *Lutheran Cyclopedia: A Concise In-Home Reference for the Christian Family*, Electronic ed. (St. Louis: Concordia, 1984). See also Schulz, *Mission from the Cross*, 163–64.

CHAPTER THREE

THE ROAD TO SOATANANA

Yes, there are Christians who are really possessed and oppressed by demons. However, when I say Christians, I am speaking about those who do not live out the faith they claim to possess. These are usually those who are Christian by only birth, or name; they belong to the Christian culture, but not to the Faith.

—A Malagasy Lutheran pastor and exorcist

To be sure, not all people think alike. We all come from different backgrounds and various cultures. This is just as true for the Christians of Madagascar as it is for the Christians of Europe, China, India, the Americas, or anywhere Christians reside in the world, including the closest neighbor to the island of Madagascar, the continent of Africa. This chapter will compare and contrast the African and Malagasy worldviews, providing a context for the reader for the forthcoming chapters that present the conversion stories and their corresponding experience with demon possession and exorcism.

The Malagasy people view the world in a much different way than the western peoples. Their worldview is religious in nature, viewing almost everything differently than we do in the West. However, there remains a point of commonality with all societies and worldviews. For the Malagasy, all experiences, including disease, sickness, and death have spiritual causes.[1] Many times disease and

---

[1] Garth D. Ludwig, *Order Restored: A Biblical Interpretation of Health, Medicine, and Healing* (St. Louis: Concordia Academic Press, 1999), 43.

death represent a direct assault upon the individual by spiritual forces. While such things should be obvious to the Christian, it is no longer the case for most of western society. Therefore, there is much to learn from our brothers and sisters in Africa. In this section, the learning process begins. First, a short warning: what you are about to read may be difficult for some to understand or believe. The worldview presented in the next few pages will seem strange and at times unbelievable to many readers. At the same time, many may find similarities to a spiritual view becoming prevalent in the post-modern world of the twenty-first century. If you doubt this assertion, simply read the news headlines of your local newspapers with a critical eye. While writing this book, the bones of a ritual sacrifice were found in a local cemetery just a few miles from my home in Michigan. The local news identified the bones as coming from an African religious ritual, probably focused on voodoo worship. While Africa and Madagascar seem like strange and faraway places, the world in which we now live has become much smaller than many of us could ever have imagined. Moreover, even our neighbors visit the local fortuneteller, read the horoscope page in the newspaper, and attend *séances* that seek to reach departed friends, lovers, and family members. Consequently, as we begin a journey into faraway places, we may soon find they are not as far away as we may have expected.

FIRST IMPRESSIONS

My experience into this strange world of paganism, exorcism, and the freedom provided by Jesus began with an interview of a pastor located 40 kilometers outside of the Malagasy city of Fianarantsoa. The trip from the capital city of Antananarivo to Fianarantsoa is difficult. One road connects the two cities. The road is about the size of neighborhood surface streets. Long sections of the road consist of only dirt, mud, and trenches that would devour a small car. However, the 40 kilometer drive to the historic *Fifohazana toby* (camp dedicated to healing) called Soatanana was considerably worse. In fact, Soatanana is only accessible by car during the dry season because of the road conditions. During other times of the year, people find it necessary to walk the distance.

3. A view of the Lutheran church located at the historic Soatanana *toby*.

4. A typical residence at a *toby* outside the city of Antsirabe.

As we approached the *toby*, the Norwegian built steeple could be seen notably against the green background of the mountains that surrounded the camp. This site began as a mission outpost of the Norwegian Lutherans in 1840. As we grew closer to the gates of the camp, men and women dressed in white gowns were noticeable behind the fence. This was my first encounter with the *mpiandry* (shepherds) of the *Fifohazana*.

The *Fifohazana* movement originated with a man named Dada Rainisoalambo. Missionaries of the London Mission Society (LMS) baptized him and trained him to be a pastor. However, when he found there was no money to be gained as a Christian pastor, he decided to return to his work as an *ombiasy* (diviner). After a few years away from the church, he and his family became ill. Large boils appeared on his skin, and his family suffered in similar ways. Yet, Rainisoalambo refused to trust in the Christian God. He sought answers from the ancestors, but no help came to them. One evening, as he was sleeping, he had a dream. In this dream, he saw a man of light telling him to quit his ancestral religion, destroy his idols, and follow Jesus. Upon waking, he destroyed all of his magical tools and returned to church, this time with his family, friends, and patrons.[2]

Rather than returning to the Reformed Church of the LMS, he began attending the Lutheran Church established by the Norwegian Mission Society (NMS). When he arrived at the church, he was dismayed that the missionaries did not know how to respond to his illness or his dream. The Lutherans had not been trained to deal with such things. Nevertheless, they prayed for Rainisoalambo and his family, and within a short time, he and his family were healed. Rainisoalambo trusted the Lord and sold all that he had so he could establish the Soatanana *toby* to be used as an evangelist outpost and camp of healing. This was the beginning of the revival movement (*Fifohazana)* in Madagascar. It was at Soatanana that Rainisoalambo trained eight men (some say twelve) whom he would call apostles. He would put these men through aggressive training that included training in humility, purity, prayer, and reading the Bible. Moreover, he instructed his apostles to remain within the church structure and work with the pastors to help them deal with the problems they were encountering. Following their training, these men were sent out to help establish churches and speak the Gospel message throughout the countryside. Prior to the apostles leaving, Rainisoalambo gave them specific instructions as to how they were to conduct themselves when confronted by the traditional religions, which included those who were oppressed or possessed by demons. He ordered them not to replicate the preachers in the churches. Rainisoalambo thought the

---

[2] Lesley A. Sharp, *The Possessed And The Dispossessed: Spirits, Identity, And Power In A Madagascar Migrant Town* (Berkeley: University of California Press, 1993), 256.

missionary pastors were good preachers who did a nice job preaching the power of Jesus' name, but he felt they lacked the resolve to cast out sickness and demons. He instructed his apostles to preach boldly and to assist the NMS missionaries in recognizing the signs that would accompany the powerful preaching of the Word. In the coming years, three additional leaders would come to the forefront of the *Fifohazana* movement. Each would establish *toby's* like the one created in Soatanana by their predecessor Rainisoalambo. The following is a list of revival movements in historic order by leader.

- Dada Rainisoalambo from Soatanana (revived in 1895)
- *Neny* Ravelonjanahary from Manolotrony (1927—Reformed Church)
- *Nenilava* from *Ankarmalaza* (1942)
- *Dadatoa* Rakotozandry from Farihimena (1946)

5. Lutheran shepherds gathering at the historic Ankarmalaza *toby* for the yearly meeting of the *Fifohazana.*

Today, the shepherd movement remains a lay program for the training of both Malagasy men and women who will assume leadership roles in the church. The white robes they wear, some at all times and others only during religious events, easily identify the shepherds to the community. These robes are not merely liturgical vestments, but outward reminders of the forgiveness they have received through the blood of Jesus. The shepherds now believe they have been given the opportunity to live their lives free from the condemnation of sin and instead for the benefit of Christ and neighbor. Therefore, all of their time and energy is dedicated to that end.

6. Lutheran church at the historic Ankarmalaza *toby*.

7. Dadatoa Rakotozandry, founder and pastor of the Farihimena *toby*.

8. Lutheran church at the historic Farihimena *toby*.

These were the men and woman behind the fence of the Soatanana *toby*. Upon our arrival, the pastor of the *toby* met us at the gate and provided us with a tour of the grounds. His name was Pastor Randrianandrasana. He had served this congregation and *toby* for more than twenty years. During the tour, we met a man sitting on the ground. He was staring at us with a strange and jagged smile. He was not dressed in the white robes that adorned the other inhabitants of the camp. As we walked by the smiling man he asked, "Hello, how are you today?" Amazed that he was speaking English, I began a conversation with him. He explained that he had learned English at the university where he had studied to be an engineer. I asked him why he was here in this remote place. His response shocked me. He said "I am here to receive freedom from the demons that torment me. I have been here for six months receiving exorcism daily and learning about the Christian faith." I was speechless. How does one without any frame of reference to such things respond to such remarks? I would soon begin to understand. What I would learn would change my own worldview and by the end of this book may change yours also.

Following the tour of the *toby*, I joined the pastor in his office. It was located toward the back of the church. This interview would be the first of many I would conduct over the next two years. This unedited interview is provided so the reader may enter this subject in the same way that I did.

INTERVIEW OF PASTOR RANDRIANANDRASANA

AUTHOR: What is your name?

PASTOR R: Pastor Randrianandrasana.

AUTHOR: How long have you been a pastor?

PASTOR R: I have been a pastor since 1987.

AUTHOR: How many exorcisms have you performed over the years?

PASTOR R: Too many to count. I have been conducting exorcisms since I became a pastor. This is very common in our church and all pastors share this experience.

AUTHOR: Are you currently working with those who are troubled persistently by spiritual forces or involved with any exorcisms?

PASTOR R: Yes, I am currently working with fifteen individuals who are demon possessed here at the *toby*.

AUTHOR: What is the cause of this possession? Was it something they did, something they asked for, or something that just came upon them?

PASTOR R: This depends upon each individual case. Some have desired the devil to enter into them. They do this hoping that they will be given the gift of prophecy, fortune-telling, healing, or talking to the ancestors. This enables them to make a good living serving the traditional religions. Another reason some are possessed is because they are unfaithful to the Christian faith. Others are possessed for reasons that we do not know.

AUTHOR: Are you saying that baptized Christians can be oppressed, or even possessed, by demons? How could Satan or his demons have dominion over a child of God?

PASTOR R: Yes, there are Christians who are really possessed and oppressed by demons. However, when I say Christians, I am speaking about those who do not live out the faith they claim to possess. These are usually those who are Christian by only birth, or name. They belong to the Christian culture, but not the Faith.

AUTHOR: Does the ancestor worship practiced by the majority of Malagasies play a part in the possessions you have encountered?

PASTOR R: Yes, of the fifteen people here at this *toby* that are possessed, at least two of them have become possessed through their interaction with the traditional religions. They beg the ancestral spirits to possess them, but these are not ancestral spirits. They are demons who disguise themselves as ancestral spirits. This is especially dangerous for those who also confess Christianity. As far as the spirits go, we call this *tromba* possession. Many people desire this type of possession because it can make them wealthy.

AUTHOR: I have read that many who have become possessed have first undergone a traumatic event in their life. Have you noticed this among the people you serve?

PASTOR R: Yes, many of them became sick through natural means such as disease or accidents; it is then, when they are in despair, that the demons come into them.

AUTHOR: When reading about possession, I have noticed different signs reported to be present in the possessed person. Have you noticed any such signs? If so, what are they?

PASTOR R: Yes, many times we see outward signs of possession. The most prominent is the ability to tell of the future or unveil hidden events. However, we also see additional signs as well; they include speaking in foreign languages that the person could not have learned, and super strength. The man you met sitting outside was possessed when he was brought here. He had such strength that we were required to keep him chained at all times because he continued to try to kill everyone.

AUTHOR: Is this man still possessed?

PASTOR R: No, would you like to continue to speak with him following our interview?

AUTHOR: Yes, I would.

PASTOR R: I will properly introduce you to him following our interview.

AUTHOR: Thank you. Continuing on, do demons speak through these possessed people?

PASTOR R: Yes, the devil does this.

AUTHOR: Do you mean the devil or demons?

PASTOR R: Yes, there are many different devils or demons who speak through the possessed people.

AUTHOR: Have you had any experience with someone who was freed from the demons through exorcism and then became possessed again?

PASTOR R: Yes, many people have the demons return to them when the people return to their old sinful lives and practices.

AUTHOR: Do the re-burial practices of the traditional religions also add to this problem?

PASTOR R: Yes, this practice is very difficult for even Christians to avoid because it is so much a part of our culture. If someone fails to participate in such an event, that person is cast away from his or her family forever. Therefore, many of the Christians continue to take part in the traditional sacrifices at the tombs. This is extremely dangerous for Christians.

AUTHOR: Can a possessed person go to church and even take part in the reception of the Lord's Supper?

PASTOR R: Yes, there are some who are baptized and worship in the church, which includes receiving the Holy Communion, who are demon possessed.

AUTHOR: This seems hard to believe. Would not the devil flee from the body and blood of Jesus?

PASTOR R: Yes, and in my experience the demons do flee, but they also return. Those demons, which do not flee, are the ones that make themselves known to us during the service by their cries and screams of agony.

AUTHOR: How does Baptism fit into exorcism?

PASTOR R: First, if a non-Christian were to come to us possessed by a demon, he would be taught the Bible. Second, exorcisms would take place, daily if necessary, and when the person was healed, they would then be baptized. Sometimes these things might occur on the same day. At other times, they may occur over a series of months. It depends upon the situation.

AUTHOR: Would this practice differ with children?

PASTOR R: Yes, we would baptize them first and then instruct them as they grow.

AUTHOR: When you use the word *exorcism*, what do you mean? Is exorcism understood as a ritual or liturgical rite? What words are spoken?

PASTOR R: We cast out the devils by the name of Jesus Christ and command them to depart into the abyss from where they came. As far as ritual prayers, such as the Roman ritual, no, we do not do this. It only distracts from the real power of Jesus' Word.

AUTHOR: Thank you very much for your time. May I use your name when I write about this?

PASTOR R: Yes, please do so.

There are many things in this interview which will no doubt cause the reader uneasiness and difficulty. This Malagasy pastor has answered differently than many of us might have expected. One of the most controversial aspects of this interview, for the western Christian, might be the pastor's acceptance of the possibility for a Christian to become possessed. However, as the reader continues through part two of this book he or she will learn that such a possibility has been accepted by the Church throughout history.

The preceding interview provides a glimpse into the exorcistic practices of the Malagasy Lutheran Church. Later, we will enter the mind of the possessed and hear the stories of many who have been freed from the bondage of Satan. However, before continuing into the possessed mind we must learn a bit from Madagascar's African neighbors. The remainder of this chapter examines the traditional African and Malagasy worldviews by demonstrating the similarities and differences of these two relatively close neighbors. The intention is to prepare the reader for the later stories of spiritual warfare.

THE TRADITIONAL AFRICAN WORLDVIEW

The African worldview is holistic. The word *holistic* has many understandings, both positive and negative depending on one's point of view. Therefore, we will define the holistic African worldview with the help of missiologist Cyril Okorocha. Okorocha describes four markers that represent the holistic nature of African tribal religions.[3] First, there is no distinction between the sacred and the secular in the African mind. Second, traditional African religion is pragmatic. For the traditional African, religion is only helpful if it serves a practical purpose (for instance, can it answer the questions and the problems of the day?). Third, traditional African religion is communally based. Africans find their individual meaning in the community.[4] Finally, African religion is power-centered. The African expects his religion to be useful; otherwise it will be rejected, and an alternative will be sought.[5] Therefore, power encounters are considered necessary within African religious systems. For the African, everything is about power. This was especially true for many of the early Christian converts.[6] Missiologist Benedict Ssettuuma differs somewhat from Okorocha by defining four different aspects to the African worldview. Ssettuuma's findings include the necessity of reality, solidarity or communality, the sacred, and anthropocentrism. Ssettuuma describes African religious realities as "dynamic actions that closely relate to everyday life."[7] The life force of a community comes from power. This leads to Ssettuuma's next point. Power resides in life, but this life is a communal event, which includes both the seen and the unseen. Once again, there is no separation between the secular and the sacred (Ssettuuma 3rd point). There is no abstract in the African religious mind; even good and evil are determined in relation to life. On this point, Ssettuuma and Okorocha agree. Whatever brings and supports life is good and whatever takes away life is evil.[8] It is necessary to keep up close relations with all human or spiritual entities so that one's life may be beneficial. Finally, Ssettuuma describes what he means by anthropocentrism, that is, all of African traditional religion is human centered. It must promote

---

[3] Cyril C. Okorocha, "Religious Conversion in Africa: Its Missiological Implications," *Missions Studies* 9, no. 2 (1992): 168–69.

[4] James E. Lassiter, "African Culture And Personality: Bad Social Science, Effective Social Activism, Or A Call To Reinvent Ethnology?" *African Studies Quarterly*, http://web.africa.ufl.edu/asq/v3/v3i3a1.htm (accessed June 24, 2010).

[5] Okorocha, "Religious Conversion in Africa," 171.

[6] Okorocha, "Religious Conversion in Africa," 174.

[7] Benedict Ssettuuma, "Mission as Service to Life: Reflections from an African Worldview," *Exchange* 33, no. 2 (2004): 182.

[8] Ssettuuma, "Mission as Service to Life," 183.

human welfare and provide answers for life's daily problems in order to be acceptable to the traditional African mind.[9]

AFRICAN ANIMISM OR POWER RELIGION

Africa is a tremendous place full of diverse people groups. Therefore, it might seem naive to present a general African understanding of traditional religion. However, studies have shown that there is a distinct thread of consistency between almost all Africans. One study, which included over 270 different people groups in Africa, concluded that all those in the study maintained a basic religious belief, one that is animistic or power centered.[10] The animistic worldview accepts a supreme creator god, who is unreachable by the living. In addition, hosts of other spiritual entities, which include ancestral spirits, exist as intermediaries. Therefore, the African perceives three dimensions within the world: the sky, the earth, and the ancestral or spirit world.[11] Moreover, for the traditional African, nothing can happen in the world that has not been ordered by the spiritual world.[12] There is an invisible world, which is the domain of spirits, and these spirits influence every aspect of life. These forces may be encouraged to act positively or negatively toward humanity through service and acts of sacrifice.[13] This causes people to seek out the spirits in the hopes of receiving power. If one can establish a proper relationship with the spirits, one can seek their influence in areas of both knowledge and prosperity. Does this sound like anything familiar? While the African mind is different from our own, in many ways it is the same. What is the difference of seeking out the hidden knowledge of the spirits or reading the horoscope pages of the newspapers? What is the difference of seeking prosperity through the guise of the spirits or from the local fortuneteller? While Africa is far from the West in terms of geography, many of the spiritual themes found in Africa can be found in western countries. This will become

---

[9] Ssettuuma, "Mission as Service to Life," 183.

[10] Keith Ferdinando, *The Triumph of Christ in African Perspective (Paternoster Theological Monographs)* (Grand Rapids: Paternoster, 1969), 27.

[11] Kalu Ogbu, "Preserving a Worldview: Pentecostalism in the African Maps of the Universe," *Pneuma* 24, no. 2 (Fall 2002): 119.

[12] Ogbu, "Preserving a Worldview," 122.

[13] Ferdinando, *The Triumph of Christ*, 1.

more apparent in the next section as we focus on the African cult of the ancestors.

The Cult of the Ancestors

Have you ever flipped through the travel and science channels of your cable television? If you have, you have no doubt noticed an increase in the number of television programs dedicated to haunted houses, ghosts, and spiritualism. One such program chronicles modern ghost hunters as they enter the homes of those oppressed by the supposed spirits of the dead. Generally, the spirits of the dead are encouraged to move on and enter the spirit world where there is peace for all. Other popular programs seek to speak to the dead and reestablish previous relationships or provide comfort for those who mourn. These programs are nothing more than forms of ancestor worship, that is, they attempt to seek help or knowledge from the dead. Many of us do these things without ever noticing the problematic nature of our actions. No, not you, you say? Have you ever visited the cemetery and placed flowers upon the grave of a loved one or close friend while speaking to them? Have you found yourself speaking aloud to a deceased spouse, mother, father, brother or sister, grandmother or grandfather? Have you ever prayed to the Virgin Mary or any of the saints? If you have, you have more in common with African animism than you may have thought. While this is true of many western thinking people, those within the scientific community, and many times the missionary community, have overlooked these similarities and even denied them.

David Burnett finds most western missionaries deficient when it comes to understanding the importance of the ancestors in the African mind. For the traditional African, family includes both the living and the dead. Those who die simply enter another plane of existence that remains connected to the daily life of the family. The ancestors have ceased to live in the flesh, but continue in spirit, free from the restrictions of the fleshly world and in closer proximity to the spirits and creator God. This provides the ancestors with superior power and influence over the daily lives of their earthly families.[14] The people seek power from the ancestors; this is the basis for their relationship.

---

[14] David Burnett, *Unearthly Powers: A Christian's Handbook on Primal and Folk Religions* (Nashville: Oliver Nelson, 1992), 60–61.

Burnett warns that this relationship not only brings the possibility of blessings and good fortune, but also misfortune, sickness, and death if the ancestors are not properly venerated.[15] If one successfully manages the ancestors, one can receive many benefits. But for those who fail to acknowledge and provide for their ancestors, there may be negative consequences.

Where are the ancestors? Where do they live? What do they do? Missiologist Robert Schreiter answers these questions in his book, *Faces of Jesus in Africa*. According to Schreiter, the ancestors live alongside the rest of the family and retain their standing within the family. A man remains a man and a woman remains a woman. Likewise, a king remains a king and those who were poor remain poor. The only difference is now their lives continue without end, only their bodies have changed.[16] Yet, for the living, the influence of the ancestors increases upon their deaths. While they carry on in much the same way in death that they did in life, they have now moved closer to the supreme deity and can act as intercessors on behalf of the living.[17]

How do the people remain in contact with their ancestors? Sometimes, it has been reported, the ancestors come to visit a person as he sleeps.[18] Missiologist Allan Anderson describes reports of ancestors appearing to their families through dreams and visions, as warnings for maltreatment. It is essential that the ancestors' instructions be carried out properly, or they will discipline their earthly relatives.[19] By keeping a positive relationship with one's ancestors, the traditional African expects to escape many misfortunes that might otherwise come upon him.[20]

---

[15] Burnett, *Unearthly Powers*, 61.

[16] Robert J. Schreiter, *Faces of Jesus in Africa* (Maryknoll, NY: Orbis Books, 1991), 119.

[17] Schreiter, *Faces of Jesus in Africa*, 119.

[18] Burnett, *Unearthly Powers*, 61.

[19] Allan H. Anderson, "Exorcism and Conversion to African Pentecostalism," *Exchange* 35, no. 1 (2006): 127.

[20] Nyakwawa U. Usiwa, "Chipembedzo Cha Makolo Achikuda (African Ancestors' Religion): Intellectualistic and Nationalistic Traits," in *African Ancestors Religion. Chipembedzo cha Makolo Achikuda*, ed. J. C. Chakanza, vol. 21 (Hauppauge: Kachere Series, 2006), 67.

9. An altar to the ancestors in Madagascar.

10. An outdoor sacrificial area dedicated to the veneration of the Malagasy ancestors.

Another way to understand the relationship between Africans and their ancestors is harmony. It is extremely crucial to retain harmony in one's life. All of life must be kept within a harmonious balance with the ancestors and spiritual forces of the universe. This requires faithful and obedient veneration of all entities of the spirit world beginning first with one's ancestors.[21] When this harmony is ruptured, Africans, many times even Christian Africans tend to revert to their traditional practices. This is usually accomplished through a diviner found within the community.[22] The diviner helps to restore the harmony between the person and his ancestral spirits by determining what has breached the harmonious relationship between the two. Many times spirit possession will accompany this harmonious reestablishment.

IMPLICATIONS OF THE AFRICAN WORLDVIEW

The holistic nature of the African mind remains difficult for western missionaries to comprehend. Generally, one finds two different reactions from the missionaries when confronted with this worldview. On the one hand, they would simply overlook the holistic/animistic worldview of the people and disregard any thoughts of a spiritual world. On the other hand, they might accept wholesale the spiritual worldview of the people and turn it into a form of Christian animism.[23]

Either one of these extremes is problematic. The first extreme forces a trench between the people and the missionaries. They simply cannot understand one another. Missiologist and well-known author Paul Hiebert describes this disconnect as the "flaw of the excluded middle."[24] Most western Christian missionaries fully believe in a religious realm of life. They believe in the triune God, angels, and demons, but they also believe there is a separation between that realm and the scientific realm. Therefore, while they teach people about the creator God (something they already believe) and about Jesus as the Savior from death, they offer little help or explanation for the people's daily problems of hunger, sickness, and death.[25] The result is

---

[21] Ferdinando, *The Triumph of Christ*, 34.

[22] Ferdinando, *The Triumph of Christ*, 39. See also Schulz, *Mission from the Cross*, 140.

[23] Pierre Gilbert, "Further Reflections on Paul Hiebert's: The Flaw of the Excluded Middle" *Direction* 36, no. 2 (Fall 2007): 210.

[24] Paul G. Hiebert, "The Flaw of the Excluded Middle," *Missiology* 10, no. 1 (January 1982): 35–47.

[25] "Traditional cultures have always understood sickness from the perspective of cosmic disorder and are much closer to the biblical sense than we in the Western world who insist that disease is something that only individuals suffer." Garth D.

syncretism; the people look to modern medicine for illnesses, but if those medicines fail, they return to the "traditional ways" of seeking help from the spirits or ancestors.

However, the problem of accepting the African worldview wholesale should be apparent. Jesus Christ is our only intermediary between the Father and us. To assume that sub-realms of spirits or ancestors are necessary to receive help from God is anything but Christian. Moreover, it prevents the African from escaping the ever-tightening yoke of sacrifice and service, which the spirits require. As a result, many Africans find themselves connecting with evil spirits who mask themselves as familiar ancestors, previous kingly figures, and helpful deities. Paul provides direction in such cases as he warns, "Satan disguises himself as an angel of light. So it is no surprise if his servants, also, disguise themselves as servants of righteousness." (2 Corinthians 11:14–15). Satan continues to disguise himself in our culture just as he does in others. He does this through the means of fortune-tellers, spiritualists, the New Age, and the like. May Jesus through the action of His Holy Word protect us and enlighten us so that we may not be misled through the deceptive ways of the devil.

Ludwig, *Order Restored: A Biblical Interpretation of Health, Medicine, and Healing* (St. Louis: Concordia Academic Press, 1999), 27.

CHAPTER FOUR

THE MALAGASY WORLD

Through exorcism, the church is always a fighting church at the forefront of the battle and at the same time a church in mission. Forgiveness of sin, liberation from the devil and his kingdom, healing from incomprehensible diseases and escaping from death are no more mere portals and empty words just to comfort someone in difficult times and posture. They become historically real and in the flesh in the life of the person through exorcism.

—Pastor Joseph Randrianasolo

One of my most memorable experiences in Madagascar occurred when I decided to explore a traditional worship site devoted to *doany* worship. The *doany* are the royal ancestral spirits of the past. This sacrificial ground proved to be quite difficult to locate. While it is located in the capital city of Antananarivo, there are no signs or other markings to identify its location to outsiders. However, a recent convert to Christianity known to my guide had previously offered many sacrifices in this location. After some conversation, he was persuaded to provide us with directions. However, he refused to accompany us to the location.

The sacrificial area was located on the edge of a rice field along the face of the tallest mountain in the area. We exited the car and followed a path down the side of a cliff. Accompanying me were Dr. Joseph Randrianasolo and our driver. As we entered the area, it was obvious that the time of sacrifice had recently concluded. Half-dried blood still dripped over the many sacrificial rocks set apart for worship. The remains of half-burnt cigarettes could be found setup as offerings to the spirits. A few straggling worshipers could be seen offering money to the spirit guardian, who turned out to be a deacon in the syncretistic reformed church of Madagascar. This was no doubt an evil place. As we entered deeper into the abyss of paganism, a heaviness came upon me that is difficult to explain. As we continued to tour the site, I prayed the Lord's Prayer under my breath for comfort and protection. Let me be clear, I simply thought the events were causing me personal anxiety. After taking a few pictures, we returned to the car and began to drive away. As soon as we began to depart, the feeling of heaviness left me, and I regained my composure. Before I had an opportunity to speak to my guide I noticed that he was conversing with the driver in Malagasy. The driver was clearly shaken. When they had finished their conversation, I told Dr. Randrianasolo of my distress. What he said to me caught me off guard. He told me that both of them had experienced similar difficulties, and he had been assuring the driver that everything was all right. He went on to say that he had experienced such feeling many times throughout his work as an exorcist. While I understand many who have not experienced such things will question this story, I will never forget this event. Moreover, many traditional Malagasies experience this distress throughout their lives, but without the protection and assurance found in Jesus. This chapter will continue where the previous chapter left off by describing the Malagasy worldview and its connections to the African worldview already presented.

Entering the Malagasy Worldview

The Malagasy worldview is similar to the African context, in that it is traditionally animistic, or power-based. Much of this relates to the geographic closeness which Madagascar shares with Africa. The Malagasy people have many deities and veneration rituals in common with African Traditional Religion. The first of these similarities comes in the form of their traditional worship practices. However, some of these worship practices, such as the *famadihana* service (re-burial and re-wrapping of ancestors' remains, which is required of many who participate in the traditional religion of Madagascar), find their genesis in Borneo, the place of origin for the majority of the Malagasy tribes.[1]

THE SPIRIT WORLD OF MALAGASY TRADITIONAL RELIGION

The Supreme Deity and Lesser Gods

The Malagasy and African worldviews are not as strange to us as they might seem at first. Almost everyone has heard of Deism. Most of the founding fathers of the United States were followers of Deism. The deistic worldview accepts a creator god. However, a deist would deny miracles and the historic interaction of God with man. God created the universe to run much like a clock that once started continues to operate without additional manipulation. An animist, wherever they may be found, in Africa, China, Madagascar, or any other part of the world would also accept the existence of a creator god. A case could be made that describes Deism as simply animism influenced by rationalism, but we will leave this topic for others to debate. One thing is clear—while there are many gods and spiritual forces in the traditional Malagasy worldview, there remains a supreme deity that is outside of the reach of humanity. In Madagascar, the creator god is known by the name *zanahary*.

Jørgen Ruud, a distinguished anthropologist and Lutheran pastor who spent more than twenty years serving as a missionary to Madagascar (1934–1954), describes the *zanahary* as the creator god who is above all other spirits. In Malagasy, his name means "he who has caused to exist."[2] He is a deity who comes and goes as he wills and can provide both blessings and misfortune as he decides. Yet he remains extremely capricious and unpredictable. If he is in a good mood, he provides riches, but when he is angry he provides curses and misfortune.

Zanahary is in many ways thought to be similar to the creator God known in Christianity.[3] However, there is no direct contact

---

[1] Ron Emoff, *Recollecting from the Past: Musical Practice and Spirit Possession on the East Coast of Madagascar (Music Culture)* (Middletown: Wesleyan, 2002), 19.

[2] Jørgen Ruud, *Gods and Ancestors: Society and Religion Among the Forest Tribes in Madagascar* (Oslo: Solum Forlag, Distributed in the U.S.A. by International Specialized Book Services, 2002), 176.

[3] Other names for *Zanahary* include *Andriamanitra* (the sweet-smelling prince), *Andriamanahary* (King or noble), *Andriantompo* (The noble one who is lord),

35

between *zanahary* and the individual.[4] Herein lies the problem; he is a far-off god who acts as he wills, but is inaccessible to the living. Moreover, he has a host of lesser gods who act in assisting him in his rule. At this point, the nature of *zanahary* becomes somewhat complicated.

The word *zanahary* can also be used to describe some of the lesser gods who also had a hand in the creation. Sometimes the name *zanahary*, when used for lesser deities, is written with a small letter and a definite article. Moreover, the name is also used by the traditional Malagasy to describe a plethora of other deities, ancestors, and spirits. The Malagasy divides these lesser deities into four categories: the gods of nature, the gods of fertility and happiness, gods with particular qualifications and functions and sacred animals.[5] If this were not enough, there is an additional category, which does not fit into the realm of either abode of the gods or the ancestors."[6] Joseph Randrianasolo provides help understanding these spirits:

> There are many kinds of spirits of the dead, but they can be categorized into two classes: the bad ones and the good ones. Among the bad ones, we can enumerate; *angatra* (ghosts), the *vazimba* (former inhabitants of the land), the *lolo* and *matoatosa* (ghosts) and the *fanahy ratsy* (bad spirits).[7]

These spirits cause many problems among the people, which include spirit-possession. They are associated with specific places and many people worship them. Randrianasolo continues:

> The *angatra*, *lolo*, and *fanahy ratsy* are spirits that harm those who trespass their territories, which may be deep ponds, waterfalls, thick bushes and so on. Sometimes these locations are situated around existing or former tombs. Usually, any harmful happenings outside of one's house, which are hard to

---

Andriananano (He who has made), *Andrianamboatra* (He who has created), and *Ratsimanamboina* (He who has no guilt). Ruud, *Gods and Ancestors*, 176–79.

[4] Alan D. Rogers, "Human Prudence and Implied Divine Sanctions In Malagasy Proverbial Wisdom," *Journal of Religion in Africa* 15, no. 3 (1985): 218.

[5] Ruud, *Gods and Ancestors*, 191–95.

[6] Ruud, *Gods and Ancestors*, 190.

[7] Joseph Randrianasolo, "Spiritual And Traditional Beliefs In The Malagasy Lutheran Church: An Analysis of Fifohazana," 2008, MS, Pretoria, 9.

explain, are attributed to the *angatra* and *lolo*. On the contrary, the *matoatosa* haunts houses, cars, and other things that the dead had used during their lifetimes. The *vazimba* are related to the tombs of former inhabitants of the land. They carry the reputation of being mean and ill-intentioned. Unlike the *lolo, angatra, matoatosa,* and *vazimba* are worshiped by some people.[8]

Another very troubling water spirit, commonly referred to by the name *ambirorandrano,* possesses young boys and draws them into the water. Many of these boys never recover mentally from this experience.[9] I have uncovered a number of these stories in my interviews. Moreover, this is a common experience expressed throughout Africa and other parts of the world. Generally, western people would know these spirits as mermaids. However, these mermaids are much different from the young pretty women who have become cartoons for children. Throughout the world, mermaids continue to be feared by many who believe in their existence.

The spirits, which are most commonly associated with spirit-possession, come under the disguise of *tromba, doany, bilo,* and *helo.* Ron Emoff has done some of the most extensive research into the *tromba* possession. He finds the word *tromba* to have several meanings. It sometimes refers to foreign royal ancestral spirits, which possess mediums; however, at other times the word can refer to a host of other spirits. *Tromba* can also refer to the possession ceremony or the medium that the spirit possesses.[10] Lesley Sharp has done a considerable amount of research into the area of *tromba* possession. She finds the majority of *tromba* mediums to be female; yet there are exceptions.[11] While *tromba* spirits are generally perceived to be

---

[8] Randrianasolo, "Spiritual And Traditional Beliefs In The Malagasy Lutheran Church," 9.

[9] Ruud, *Gods and Ancestors*, 190.

[10] Emoff, *Recollecting from the Past*, 2.

[11] Lesley A. Sharp, *The Possessed and the Dispossessed: Spirits, Identity, and Power in a Madagascar Migrant Town (Comparative Studies of Health Systems and Medical Care)* (New York: University of California Press, 1996), 123.

helpful spirits by the people, they can be extremely dangerous to the person who rejects their wishes.[12]

Tromba, doany, bilo, and *helo* possessions are associated with the ancestors of the people.[13] By seeking possession people hope to gain the power that the spirits possess. This is accomplished through the healing advice that the *tromba* spirits provide as well as other secret knowledge that may be gained as a result of their presence. This provides people with answers for the problems of daily life such as sickness and misfortune.[14] The people invite these spirits to take control of their bodies. However, some spirits possess people without their invitation (*bilo,* and *helo* spirits). Many who receive this type of possession behave like animals mimicking the actions of snakes.[15]

What does a spirit attack look like? Emoff describes them as causing forceful convulsions and shaking of the body.[16] One of the most dangerous spirits identified by the traditional Malagasy believer is the *njarinintsy*. These spirits cause grave illness, and are generally associated with uncontrollable screaming and crying; many of those possessed experience loss of memory and confusion.[17] These are the spirits of Madagascar, which when improperly venerated bring great calamity upon their followers.

The Ancestors

To the Malagasy, the ancestors (*razana*) play a continual role in their lives by providing blessing or misfortune and curses.[18] The word *razana* means, "a long dead, unspecified forebear."[19] The word can also indicate a dead person or corpse in some cases.[20] Usually the

---

[12] Opoku Onyinab, "Contemporary "Witchdemonology" in Africa," *International Review of Mission* 95, no. 3701371 (October 2004): 337.

[13] Eva Keller, The *Road to Clarity: Seventh-Day Adventism in Madagascar* (New York: Palgrave Macmillan, 2005), 47.

[14] Emoff, *Recollecting from the Past*, 43.

[15] Sharp, *The Possessed and the Dispossessed*, 141.

[16] Emoff, *Recollecting from the Past*, 46.

[17] Sharp, *The Possessed and the Dispossessed*, 140.

[18] Keller, *The Road to Clarity*, 169.

[19] Joseph Randrianasolo, "Spirits in Madagascar," interview by author, August 3, 2009.

[20] Maurice Bloch, *Placing the Dead: Tombs, Ancestral Villages, and Kinship Organization in Madagascar* (Prospect Heights: Waveland Press, 1971), 112.

dead become *razana* following the completion of the traditional funeral rites.[21]

11. A traditional Malagasy tomb.
Notice a window provides the resident with a view of the family lands. The Malagasy believe the spirits of the ancestors reside in the tombs just as the living reside in their homes. Because the ancestors will live eternally in the tombs and only a short time in their earthly homes, no expense is spared on their construction.

Tombs are extremely important to the Malagasy.[22] On each of my research trips to Madagascar, I spent a considerable amount of time visiting the tombs. One cannot drive through the countryside without noticing them perched upon the hills. They are noticeable because their construction is in such contrast to the typical Malagasy home. The constructions of most countryside homes consist of sticks and mud, but the tombs are usually cement or brick. The tombs look like houses, and the houses look like tombs. What I mean is the tombs are well kept and modern looking while the homes are many times falling down and deserted looking. One tomb I observed had multiple levels and windows surrounding the large coffin placed on the upper floor providing a three-hundred and sixty-degree view of the valley for the ancestors of the tomb.

---

[21] Randrianasolo, "Spiritual And Traditional Beliefs In The Malagasy Lutheran Church," 9.

[22] For a complete account of the building of the tombs according to the traditional religion, see Jørgen Ruud, *TABOO; A Study of Malagasy Customs and Beliefs* (Oslo: Oslo University Press, 1960), 128–41.

12. This traditional Malagasy tomb looks like a home.
Those who built the tomb live in homes made of sticks, grass, and mud.

Most of the tombs found on the island are more expensive than the houses in which people live; they can be the greatest expense that one can incur during one's lifetime.[23] It is normal to spend more money on tombs than life itself because the tomb is to be the eternal abode while an earthly home has only temporal benefits.[24] There are many similarities here to what has already been described in the African ancestral understanding. The tombs are eternal homes that serve as points of connection between two worlds—the world of the living and the world of the dead. One of the greatest acts of obedience that a traditional Malagasy can show to the *razana* is the *famadihana* (burial rite of Northern tribes.)

While the word *famadihana* is foreign to most of us, the practice is not. *National Geographic* has featured this burial ritual many times as have numerous other publications and programs. The difference between this burial ritual and others is the number of times it takes place. In most cultures burial is a onetime event, but this is not so in Madagascar. The *famadihana* is preformed every few years by the

---

[23] Maurice Bloch, *Placing the Dead: Tombs, Ancestral Villages, and Kinship Organization in Madagascar*, 113.

[24] Bloch, *Placing the Dead*, 113–14.

families who will eventually be buried in the tomb. All living relatives must participate in the feast, both personally and financially, or face excommunication from the family both in this life and the next. While there are various options depending on the tribe of origin, the ritual always requires the exhumation of the body from the tomb and a rewrapping of the remains.[25]

Randrianasolo describes the widespread use of the *famadihana* across Madagascar. He writes, "Nowadays, the *famadihana* is practiced all over the country even though it has remained the monopoly of the inland for many years."[26] The *famadihana* was originally associated with the *Merina* tribe, which is centrally located in the highlands. However, because they were the ruling tribe on the island for many years, they have spread out to other areas of the island. This has resulted in the spread of the *famadihana*.

Not all Malagasy tribes practice *famadihana*. Some of the tribes, which share African roots, do not follow the *famadihana*. However, their tombs remain just as important to them as to the other inhabits of the island. In place of the *famadihana,* these tribes follow a ritual called *fitampoha*. This is the ceremony followed on the coastland. The English translation of the word is "royal bath." This ceremony consists of bathing the royal relics or *dady* of the ancient kingdom of *Menabe*.[27] Randrianasolo describes the meaning of the ceremony:

> On the one hand, bathing is a sign of continuing submission and adoration of the living to the dead. He is still protecting his subjects. Now he can do these obligations in the best conditions because he is ranked among the pantheon of gods. This parallels what is occurring in the *famadihana*. In this just-mentioned ceremony, the dead will bless the living who take care of them.[28]

---

[25] Bloch, *Placing the Dead*, 145.

[26] Randrianasolo, "Spiritual and Traditional Beliefs in The Malagasy Lutheran Church," 11.

[27] Eléonore Nerine Botokeky, "Le Fitampoha en Royaume de Menabe, in Les Souverains de Madagascar," trans. Joseph Randrianasolo, in *L'Histoire Royale et se Résurgences Contemporaines*, ed. Françoise Raison-Jourde (Paris: Karthala, 1983), 211.

[28] Randrianasolo, "Spiritual and Traditional Beliefs in The Malagasy Lutheran Church," 12.

One thing that both *famadihana* and *fitampoha* have in common is spirit-possession. Spirit possession is one of the common links between all Malagasy tribes.[29] More than 50 percent of the inhabitants of the island still follow the traditional religion, namely animism. This fact, along with the common phenomenon of spirit-possession, explains the situation found within the Malagasy Lutheran Church and the high number of exorcisms it performs.

SPIRITUAL WARFARE, EXORCISM, AND CONVERSION IN THE MALAGASY LUTHERAN CHURCH

Now that we have established the basic framework of the Malagasy worldview, we will get to the heart of this book: how spiritual warfare, exorcism, and conversion fit into the Malagasy context. This section will demonstrate the significance of exorcisms that take place in connection with a movement called the Fifohazana movement. Randrianasolo describes the place of the Fifohazana movement within the Malagasy Lutheran Church:

> The Malagasy Lutheran Church has seven branches of communities. The community of the *Fifohazana* is one of them. A community is the ensemble of all members of a branch in the Malagasy Lutheran Church. The constitution of the Malagasy Lutheran Church states, 'The community of the *Fifohazana* preaches the gospel to all people, especially to the gentiles through the activities of the *Fifohazana* in their respective church, *toby,* and surrounding areas.' It practices two kinds of mission: the inside and the outside. The inside mission targets Christians who combine ancestor worship under its various aspects as above described and mentioned with their Christian beliefs. The outside mission aims at winning gentiles or non-Christian persons for the faith in Jesus Christ, the Son of God. Briefly stated, the *Fifohazana* works through and for the church.[30]

---

[29] Cynthia Holder-Rich, "Spirits and the Spirit: The Ministry of Madagascar's Healing Shepherds," *Religion and Theology* 13, no. 1 (2006): 55.

[30] Randrianasolo, "Spiritual and Traditional Beliefs in The Malagasy Lutheran Church," 11–15.

Because of the continued mixing of false religious beliefs with Christianity (syncretism) the Malagasy Church trusts the *Fifohazana* movement to deal with spirit-possession not only among the heathen, but also with its own members. The Malagasy Lutheran Church is currently active in removing all forms of syncretism from the lives of its members, although such a change is exceptionally difficult in an animistic culture. For example, to refrain from the burial practices of the *famadihana* and *fitampoha* usually brings excommunication from the family of origin. People, therefore, feel compelled to participate in the practices, although these practices always seek to communicate with the dead, exposing the participants to the demonic activity found in the *tromba* worship that must accompany such ceremonies. As a result, undesired possession sometimes occurs even to those who profess membership in the Church. Exorcism is not only a leading tool in the conversion of many traditional Malagasies, but also a tool necessary for the members of the church and their protection.

13. Christian converts are beginning to establish their own cemeteries to avoid the traditional burial practices associated with the *Famadihana.*

Exorcism is the answer for any demonic problems faced in this world. Many times, we might think exorcism is only necessary for an individual who has a demon possessing the physical body, but the

Malagasy Lutheran Church would criticize such pragmatic thinking. Malagasy exorcism rites should not be viewed in terms of Roman Catholic ritualistic themes or in terms of Hollywood cinema. Exorcism is not something an individual does, but the work of Jesus who drives Satan and his demons away from either person or place. Yet, exorcism is mostly understood in terms of physical possession. Therefore, Pastor Randrianasolo describes the events that usually accompany the exorcism of an individual:

> If a person is demon-possessed and hears the Word of Jesus, many times the demons throw him on the ground, convulse him, or put him in an unconscious state. Sometimes, he screams. The *mpiandry* surround him and cast out the demons until he is freed. Then they lay hands on him. Afterwards, that demon-possessed person usually gets counseling and teaching of the faith in Jesus Christ.[31]

Finally, Randrianasolo adds:

> Conversion happens before or after health recovery. Many of the healed demon-possessed persons have become *mpiandry*.[32]

This last statement leads to some questions that this book answers. What happens to a person when they undergo exorcism? What was their experience before, during and after exorcism? What did they experience in their animistic life? What are their present experiences? These questions formed the research for this book. Moreover, I suggest the answer to these questions may be helpful to western Christianity as it deals with a culture that continues to seek communications with the dead and other occult practices.

The Malagasy Lutheran Liturgy of Exorcism

Understanding the Significance of the Exorcism Liturgy

There are two forms of exorcism found in the Liturgy of the Malagasy Lutheran Church: the general exorcism of place and the

---

[31] Randrianasolo, "Spiritual and Traditional Beliefs In The Malagasy Lutheran Church," 18–19.

[32] Randrianasolo, "Spiritual and Traditional Beliefs in The Malagasy Lutheran Church," 18–19.

specific exorcism of an individual. This chapter discusses each of these rites. However, each form of exorcism has a common basis. Randrianasolo writes:

> In case of exorcism, the Name and the person of Jesus Christ occupy the center of the exorcism. From that perspective, evangelism using exorcism may be interpreted as Christ-centered evangelism. The liturgy itself comprehends a predetermined time for individual participation in loudly said prayers; verse Bible readings, short exhortations on healings, liberation from the devils and in answers of prayers. All of these are finalized by a longer preaching stressing on the power and authority of Jesus Christ of Nazareth. Then, hymn 175 from the church hymnbook asking the Holy Spirit to come and to work, is sung. It is at that time that the *mpiandry*, the Bible held against the left chest by the left hand, with their white robes (symbol of forgiveness and liberation) proceed to stand and surround the people to be exorcised. Six of those who stand in front of the people lead the exorcism one by one: the first one prays; the four next ones read successively in the gospels written by John 14:12–17; Mark 16:15–20; Matthew 18:18–20 and John 20:21–23. The specificity of these four readings is that they were taken out of Jesus' discourses in the three gospels. The sixth and last person prays or leads the exorcism itself by saying aloud, "In the Name of Jesus Christ of Nazareth, you devils, *bilo*, *tromba*, *doany*, diseases, and power of death, go out." All the standing *mpiandry* in white robes proceed around and in between the people performing exorcisms with loud voices. If there are persons who show signs of erratic or irrational behavior, many *mpiandry* come to them and concentrate their exorcism actions on them until the behavior ceases and the concerned persons pray and pronounce the Name of Jesus in their prayers.[33]

---

[33] Joseph Randrianasolo, "More Reflections upon Exorcism as a Means of Grace," e-mail message to author, June 22, 2010.

14. Following three years of training, these lay men and women are installed
into the position of *mpihandry* (shepherd). Soon they will join the ranks
of thousands of others who assist the pastors as exorcists.

In this lengthy quote, Randrianasolo identifies two possible forms
of exorcism. The first exorcism, that is, "the exorcism of place," is an
exorcism of the entire church including all those gathered for worship
(the generally assembly of the church). If a possessed person is
identified, the *mpiandry* then continue with the "specific exorcism" of
person." The exorcism of person only occurs if a demon-possessed
person is within the gathering. What follows will be a similar rite of
the exorcism of place, but this time the possessed person will be the
focus of the exorcistic words rather than the greater assembly.
Randrianasolo describes the deeper significance of this liturgy from
an insider perspective:

> These patterns in the exorcism bring to the surface the deep
> meaning flowing undercurrent. They carry a central message
> throughout the event. There is only one Lord and one Savior:
> Jesus Christ. It is a Christ-centered event. The four readings
> all combined point to the heart of the exorcism. This can be
> subdivided into five items. First, the very words of Jesus are
> the foundations of the exorcism. Second, the Holy Spirit is
> the dynamic motor of the work. Third, there is a promise of
> the answer to prayers. Fourth, forgiveness of sin is one of the

results of the exorcism. At the laying on of hands, the *mpiandry* ends his prayer with a request to Holy Spirit to provide the forgiveness of sin. Fifth, the sending out into the world is accompanied by the signs for the believers. During the exorcism itself, the Name of Jesus is the key word repeated at each casting out words. The main theme of the follow up teaching after the exorcism for those who have undergone it simply carries the exhortation to believe in Jesus Christ, the Son of God and who is the only Savior for this life and the eternal life.

Exorcism, therefore, puts the *mpiandry* and the *Fifohazana* at the forefront of a daily battle against Satan and his kingdom. Satan is like a lion roaring around us as Peter said, ready to bite and to kill. Jesus has come to conquer him, to destroy his kingdom and to establish the Kingdom of God that is no more at hand, but is right here now in His person. Consequently, exorcism cultivates in the life of the *mpiandry* and that of the *Fifohazana* a life of a continuing relationship with Jesus Christ who is the only guarantee leading to victory. Therefore, through the exorcism, the church is always fighting at the forefront of the battle and at the same time a church in mission. Forgiveness of sin, liberation from the devil and his kingdom, healing from incomprehensible diseases and escaping from death are no more mere paroles and empty words just to comfort someone in difficult times and posture. They become historically real and in the flesh in the life of the person through exorcism. These fleshly historical happenings boost and propel evangelism in an incredible way toward the heavens and give joy to the angels. In that definition, exorcism is one more exemplification of how the Lutheran Confessions present Jesus Christ. That is the dynamism in the strength of the growth of the Malagasy Lutheran Church.[34]

From these remarks, one can see that the exorcistic liturgy of the Malagasy Lutheran Church is a primary tool to employ conversion of the traditionally minded Malagasies.

---

[34] Randrianasolo, "More Reflections," e-mail message to author, June 22, 2010.

15. The Shepherds of the Lutheran Church of Madagascar
wearing their traditional white robes as they surround the crowd
preparing for a general exorcism of the gathering place.

THE GENERAL EXORCISM (AN EXORCISM OF PLACE)

Most of us are familiar with this type of exorcism even if the
actual Malagasy rite is foreign to our understandings. The Church has
retained rites of exorcism for homes and other locations throughout
time. Often this takes place through various rites of dedication or
blessing, which includes a prayer for divine protection from evil or an
outright command for Satan and his devils to depart. In the Malagasy
context, the general exorcism of place provides for such situations.
However, this form of exorcism can occur in many different contexts
including the church service. In some Malagasy churches, this form
of exorcism occurs as a portion of the pre-liturgy just prior to the
confession and absolution portion of the service. At other times, the
general exorcism may take place as a stand-alone service. Yet, in each
case, the basic ritual is identical.[35]

---

[35] I observed the exorcism ritual described in 2007 while witnessing a mass event at a
toby in the Malagasy city of Toliara.

1. The sick, including fathers, mothers, and children, gather in preparation of the service of exorcism.

2. The service begins with prayers of protection.

3. The congregation begins to sing the hymns of the church.

4. One of the pastors preaches a sermon.

5. Additional hymns asking the Holy Spirit to work amongst the assembly are sung. It is at this time that the shepherds, wearing their white robes, take their place in the area where the exorcism ceremony will be carried out.

6. Following the hymns, a number of Scriptures are read from the Gospels that deal with exorcism, forgiveness of sins, the crucifixion, and resurrection. This normally includes John 14:12–17; Mark 16:15–20; Matthew 18:18–20; and John 20:21–23.

7. The pastor repeats various areas of the previous sermon in a summary format.

8. Additional prayers of protection are said.

9. Then, the general rite of exorcism begins. The exorcistic words used are a variation of the phrase, "Depart (*mivoaka* [pronounced as *m' voaka*] *amin'ny Anaran'i Jesosy*) in the name of Jesus Christ into the abyss which you came."

10. If demonic activity is encountered, the assembly begins the rite of specific exorcism, focusing on the possessed individual. Usually it is abundantly evident if a possessed individual is present due to the loud wailing or other physical manifestations that present themselves.

11. When the exorcism of place is completed, a ceremony of prayer called the laying on of hands follows.

12. Finally, they proceed with the Divine Service (if the exorcism ceremony takes place before or at one point of the service [usually after the preaching]).

16. Thousands of Lutherans gathered outside the city
of Antsirabe, Madagascar, for general exorcism and prayer.

THE SPECIFIC EXORCISM (AN EXORCISM OF PERSON)

The exorcism of a demon-possessed person can follow a general exorcism of place if necessary. If additional exorcisms are required (sometimes many exorcisms are needed to free the possessed person from the grasp of the demons) they may take place in a shortened form within the *toby*. If the specific exorcism follows the general exorcism, the following rite is used:

1. As many pastors and shepherds as are available direct their command to depart toward the possessed individual. Some will hold the possessed person down to prevent the demon from causing harm to the body of the individual.

2. This continues until the demon appears to have left the individual. Note: many times demons will attempt to hide; also, many times there may be multiple demons within the individual. If this is the case, the weakest demons will leave first, and the exorcism will seem to proceed in waves of calmness, and then build to higher intensity as the stronger demons are confronted.

3. Throughout the exorcism, one of the pastors or shepherds will take a leadership role. As the leader, they will speak to the demonized person whenever a moment of calmness presents itself. This is done in an attempt to determine how or why the demon came to possess the person. Many of Malagasy exorcists report during this time the individuals recall how and when their possession occurred. At other times, the demon may answer the question as to how and why possession occurred. Also, during the time of calmness, the leader and possibly others who are present pray for the individual.

4. When the demons appear to be gone, and the person seems to be in their right mind, they are encouraged to pray for their own deliverance in the name of Jesus. If the demon remains, it will prevent the person from praying in Jesus' name. Note: many times a demon will allow prayer, but only in a general form that addresses god, rather than a prayer in the name of Jesus. However, it is not until the Holy Spirit gives the individual the power to make this confession and prayer that the demon will normally depart. One additional but crucial point is during the questioning and the prayers of the leader the other exorcists continue to speak the words commanding the demon to depart in the name of Jesus. The only time

the other exorcists stop their exorcistic commands is during the moments of calmness.

5. After the rite of exorcism, hymns and concluding prayers provide for comfort and protection for all involved.[36]

Additional exorcisms of the possessed usually include the following adjustments:

1. Because the possessed individual has already been identified, the general exorcism of place will not be necessary.

2. The rite begins with prayer, hymn singing, Scripture reading, and preaching.

3. The possessed individual is restrained (to prevent personal injury).

4. The rest of the rite follows the rite of specific exorcism.

5. The duration of the exorcism varies. The exorcism is considered successful when the individual regains composure and begins to pray in Jesus' name.[37]

Jesus sent His apostles out into the world to free a people that were lost in darkness. The Malagasy Lutherans have taken this command to heart as they employ this exorcistic strategy in many areas of their ministry. The next three chapters will demonstrate how this strategy has freed many people from the dark bondage of Satan through the gift of exorcism. John reminds us that it was for freedom and release that Jesus entered the world. John writes, "The reason the Son of God appeared was to destroy the works of the devil" (1 John 3:8).

---

[36] The hymn singing observed in the rite seemed to be spontaneous. No one individual announced the hymn, but those present began singing without provocation. This demonstrates the familiarity the *mpiandry* have concerning the rite.

[37] Randrianasolo remarks that a prayer in the general name of God will not be sufficient. Only a prayer in Jesus' name indicates that the evil spirit has departed.

CHAPTER FIVE

RELYING ON THE ANCESTORS AND SPIRITS

We relied upon the razana *and the* ombiasy *and we called upon them for help in everything we did. They gave us ways of how to do things, and we accepted them as true.*

—A convert to the Malagasy Lutheran Church

In preparation for this book, I was given the opportunity to present this data before a PhD class at a well-known theological seminary. The class contained PhD students from The United States, Africa, and Asia. During the presentation, I showed a video of the exorcism described in the first chapter of this book. The Americans who watched the video received it differently than those from African and Asia. The American theological students expressed disbelief and doubt about what they had seen. However, the others simply nodded their heads in agreement. The conversation that ensued demonstrates the vast differences of experience and worldviews between students. The African and Asian students spoke of similar stories, many of which included exorcisms that they had performed during their ministries at home. On the other hand, the American students had no frame of reference for such stories, except those produced through horror movies of Hollywood. This was a clash of worldviews among good and faithful Christian students. Many who read the following chapters will experience, at least in part, the situation just described. All of us come from differing backgrounds and have much to teach each other. The area of exorcism is one which the Western Church can learn much from its partner churches.

Christians come to faith at various times in life. Some are born into the faith through the gift of Baptism as infants while others may hear the life-giving Gospel at other times during their lives. The majority of those who come to faith in Madagascar do so as adults. This should not be surprising considering that the Malagasy Lutheran Church is a growing church in an area of the world where the majority of the population remains within the fold of the traditional religions. Therefore, many of the people we will encounter in this chapter share lives of deep bondage to both their deceased ancestors and the spirit world, both of which are actually demons in disguise.

This chapter seeks to describe the history of those people we will meet on the journey. All of them will answer the following questions:

1. What was your previous religious allegiance or identity?

2. Where did you look for spiritual comfort in life?

3. What exposure did you have with spiritual entities?

4. Have you ever received any form of spiritual healings?

5. Have you had any experiences with exorcism?

The purpose of this chapter is to demonstrate the bondage these people endure without the help or protection of Jesus. The material presented in the next few chapters will be challenging to the worldview of many who read them. One thought you may have is, "How can people believe such things and be held captive in such ways?" Yet, if we were to step back and look at our own situations, we might find that we, too, have experienced similar forms of bondage. While most of us have never been forced to worship the spirits or seek out secret knowledge from the dead, Satan continues to hold society in bondage in many other ways. Have you ever been addicted to drugs or alcohol? Have you ever felt chained to a slot machine or a card game? Have you felt the constant pull of pornography? The bondage of Satan and sin surround us in this life. While western bondage may appear different from those faced in Madagascar and other parts of the world, they remain bondage, and Jesus remains the only answer for the bondage of sin. In fact, we in the western world may be in a more difficult position than them. While both of our bondages are spiritual, at least their bondage is understood in a spiritual context, while our spiritual bondage is dressed in the clothing of the enlightenment and rationalistic thinking. Where others see spirits causing them pain and suffering, too often we see only natural forces and psychological illnesses. Others look for spiritual answers to spiritual problems. We can learn much from these Malagasy brothers and sisters as we attempt to understand our own circumstances. I maintain that the Malagasy understanding presented in this book is much closer to the understanding of the first century Christians than our own. Therefore, the reader will no doubt encounter stories that could just as well be found walking down the streets in biblical times as they are today in many other parts of the world, including Madagascar.

WHO ARE THESE PEOPLE AND WHAT ARE THEIR STORIES?

RELIGIOUS BACKGROUNDS

The first questions asked of our new friends sought to determine their previous religious experiences, that is, before entering the Lutheran Church. The majority of the people identified their religious backgrounds in terms of animism (seeking power and knowledge from the spiritual world). The vast majority claimed previous cultic allegiances with both the ancestors (*razana*) and the shamanistic representatives of the *razana*, i.e., the diviners (*ombiasy*). These relationships are of reciprocity. The people assume that through faithful sacrifice and adherence to the spiritual rules and requirements (taboos) they can appease the ancestors (*razana*) and spirits, thereby receiving a benefit from them rather than a curse. The *ombiasy* generally acts as intermediaries between the respondents and the *razana*. One of major benefits of this relationship was the personal blessings or secret knowledge the people believed they received from the spirits. However, in each case the underlying alliance of the people was fear-based. Before becoming Christians, the people believed that it was necessary to venerate the *razana* so calamity would not result.

The social and economic situation in Madagascar continues to have devastating effects upon the people. Madagascar remains one of the poorest countries in the world.[1] As a result, starvation, disease,

---

[1] "CIA—The World Factbook," Welcome to the CIA Web Site — Central Intelligence Agency, Economy, https://www.cia.gov/library/publications/the-world-factbook/geos/ma.html (accessed August 09, 2010).

and limited life expectancies continue to force people into a state of fear and dread. Moreover, due to their belief system they tend to spend what little income they possess adhering to the request of the *ombiasy*, *razana*, and spirits. This mystical worldview reports receiving visits from deceased elders (parents, grandparents) who prescribe the sacrifice they require in order to provide specific blessings or knowledge. This hidden or occult knowledge is sought to provide necessary answers to remove a curse or reestablish a broken relationship. However, at other times people seek knowledge to bring calamity on other individuals or groups. While the people anticipate blessings and knowledge, few actually find any lasting effects in either category.

One area the majority of people identified with was spirit-possession. The widely held belief of the people who were interviewed while researching this book thought spirit possession to be a means of bringing themselves into direct contact with the spirits. Therefore, spirit possession was highly sought after by those interviewed. Moreover, many described themselves as being previously possessed by a spiritual entity. However, all too often the people did not receive the spirits they sought after. Instead of being possessed by a *tromba* spirit (those spirits perceived to be good by the traditional Malagasy), many of the people described being possessed by one of the evil spirits and as a result, suffered much hardship. These spiritual attacks resulted in significant physical, mental, and spiritual bondage. Many people described their pre-converted lives in terms of hopelessness and depression. The next section will examine the personal stories and experiences of these people. However, it will also contain statistical data for those desiring a more detailed investigation. Those readers who are not interested in this detail may wish to scan through this section, only reading the individual stories. Whatever your interest level, this section will introduce you to the lives of Christians who have encountered the demonic and present their stories so that we might avoid similar pitfalls.

A note of caution is necessary at this point. While much of what you will encounter will be new, and at times exceedingly difficult for you to accept and understand, I encourage you to remember all of these people are now wonderful and faithful Christians—many of whom are now pastors and church leaders. Let us begin our journey into this strange world as we listen to these people tell us the stories of their lives so that we may grow together.

LIFE IN THE TRADITIONAL RELIGION OF MADAGASCAR

Question: Please describe your previous religion (Animism?).

The first question asked of those interviewed focused on their previous religious background. What was their story? As it turns out, 59 percent of those questioned had no previous attachment with Christianity. They shared the traditional religious background of animism as found on the island. The next highest group originated from a form of Roman Catholicism mixed with traditional animism (syncretism). This group accounted for 17 percent of those interviewed. The remaining people identified during the research represented a mingling of various religious backgrounds, including Islam, and other Christian affiliations.

FOCUS OF SPIRITUAL COMFORT

Question: Describe to whom you looked for spiritual/physical help or comfort (traditional diviners, ancestors, secular sources, priests, Christians, Jesus, etc.). What help did you experience?

The first part of the question seeks to identify the spiritual allegiances of the people. The research found that prior to becoming Christian the majority of those questioned sought spiritual allegiances with both the *razana* (17.2%) and *ombiasy* (60.9%). However, none of the people claimed the ability to communicate with the *razana* apart from the actions of the *ombiasy*. The only exception was when a person carried the title of *ombiasy*. These people claimed to have a direct connection to the *razana*; however, their original connection was always through the invitation of a superior *ombiasy*. The fundamental connection between the *razana* and the *ombiasy* requires the understanding that the two allegiances are essentially one combined allegiance. Therefore, 78 percent of the respondents shared the same spiritual allegiance.

The second portion of the question helps us to understand how these allegiances were beneficial to the people. In the majority of the cases, the people identified blessings they had received to be the work of the *razana*. The people who fell into this category understood the blessings that they had received as mediations between the *ombiasy* and *razana*. The following can sum up the totality of the responses:

> We relied upon the *razana* and the *ombiasy* and we called upon them for help in everything we did. They gave us ways of how to do things, and we accepted them as true.[2]

The work of the *ombiasy* is holistic and pertains to every aspect of life for the traditional Malagasy. The people saw the *ombiasy* as teachers, healers, advisors, astrologists, and priests. The *ombiasy* assist their followers in the very basic of ways to the most complex. One person spoke of the assistance he received from an *ombiasy* in removing a fish bone caught within his throat while others would describe the immense wealth and power they had received from the charms and talisman purchased from the *ombiasy*. Whatever the situation, all recognized the *ombiasy's* knowledge and power resulted from their connection to the spirit world.

PREVIOUS EXPOSURE TO SPIRITS AND ANCESTORS

Question: What, if any, experiences have you had with the spirits?

This question seeks to determine what actual interactions the people experienced with various types of spiritual entities and what benefits they received from these interactions. The primary response reported was the reception of individual blessings, with the next highest response the obtainment of hidden knowledge.

The search for blessings and fortune was the primary concern of the people. One of those questioned, an *ombiasy*, reports how he would receive blessings from the *razana*:

> I had a good relationship with the *razana* and the *tromba*. When someone came to me to request knowledge of their sickness, I would ask the *razana* to provide me with the answers by offering sacrifices of thanksgiving for supplying what I needed.[3]

---

[2] Interview S28M05.

[3] Interview S27F10.

The search for the blessings of the *razana* is all-encompassing and reaches every aspect of the traditional Malagasy life. One response summed up the majority opinion:

> We relied upon the blessings of the *razana,* and these blessings were very powerful. We respected the *razana* and the *ombiasy*. Everything we did was agreed upon beforehand with the *razana* and the *ombiasy*.[4]

Another person reported:

> I was not afraid of the *razana* because I had a good relationship with them. I spent much of my time among the tombs. I thought that by remaining close to the tombs, both day and night, I would receive blessings, but I did not. I also believed that if I did not follow what the *razana* told me to do it would lead to danger.[5]

Yet others spoke directly to the negative aspects of failing to maintain a positive relationship with the *razana*:

> When I was a pagan, the *razana* would come to torment me. I had a great fear of the *razana* and a desire for their blessings. When I kept all of their taboos life was good. This is why I respected the *razana*.[6]

A positive relationship with the *razana* requires sacrifice. These sacrifices may take many forms that included the *famadihana* (a re-burial ritual). These sacrifices would come at a high cost to the individuals. One individual describes her experience:

> One year the *ombiasy* required us to conduct the *famadihana* to insure that we had the blessings and protection of the *razana* upon our work. I spent all the money I had on that one *famadihana*. This sacrifice required me to kill twenty of my bulls for the feast. This is how I was required to give thanks to the *razana* and insure their blessings.[7]

---

[4] Interview S28M05.

[5] Interview S02F05.

[6] Interview S23M04.

[7] Interview S53F21.

While the majority of those interviewed concluded that they had received a blessing from the *razana*, they also concluded this blessing came at a high price. The desire to appease the *razana* was constantly upon the minds of the respondents, so much so that it took over almost every aspect of their lives.

RECIPIENTS OF SPIRITUAL HEALINGS

Question: Have you ever experienced any healing from the spirits? Please describe your experience.

While the previous questions were purposely broad in scope, the function of this question is to understand what the people believe they received because of their relationship with the *razana* and *ombiasy*. This question delves into the nature of the blessing received in the previous questions. It specifically focuses on the aspect of healing, which many traditional religions report providing.

Thirty-one percent responded favorably to this question. They reported actual healings taking place through the blessings of the *razana*. Moreover, a high number of those questioned who did not identify physical healing still reported various blessings received through the actions of the *razana*.

The individual responses help to illuminate the means by which healings occurred. One person replied, "Yes, I was healed. One day I was sick and about to die, but the *razana* loved me and healed me."[8] Another person spoke of the healing his child received by the *razana*, "my child was sick, so I called upon the *razana* and told them if my child would be returned to health I would offer a sacrifice. My child became well, and I offered the sacrifice of a cow."[9] Another reported:

> In 1982, my father was sick, and he was in a coma three times per day. I made a vow at the tombs of our grandparents that if they would heal my father then I would kill a cow. After six months, my father was healed, and I killed the cow to carry out my vow.[10]

---

[8] Interview S16M11.

[9] Interview S21M11.

[10] Interview S62M10.

Such stories predominate in the interviews. Many respondents claim to have received healing for themselves or their families. However, these healings came at a high price. This is evident in the following remarks:

> I knew that because of my worship and respect for the *razana* I would receive their blessings. When I was in need, I called them through the charms and talisman that I had received from the *ombiasy*. I was also able to heal other people from their sicknesses by the medicine and the sacrifices. I thought the *ombiasy* could perform many things and protect people from the *razana* and their curses. Many times these curses would lead to disease. I practiced all of this and found a place within the center of the community. However, all of the *taboos* were very heavy upon me.[11]

While many of the people (35.9%) claimed to have received healing from the *razana*, they also reported enduring enormous burdens because of the healings.

Many of those interviewed were once *ombiasy* themselves. It is therefore necessary to hear how they describe their healing abilities. One *ombiasy* describes his methods of providing healing through the *razana*:

> Yes, I received healing from the *razana*. When I used the *sikidy* (a traditional device for divination), the *razana* talked to me and advised me as to which medicine to use to heal others and myself. I was instructed to take the branches and leaves and give them to the people that approached me. Through these things, the people would receive healing.[12]

Another *ombiasy* describes how he healed his wife through the traditional methods:

> I healed people through the *razana*. My wife was very sick and about to die. I healed her by calling upon the *razana* and through the using of branches, leaves, and powder from the bones of the *razana*.[13]

---

[11] Interview S23M04.

[12] Interview S8M11.

[13] Interview S09M11.

Based on the results of this question it appears that the majority of those questioned believe in the existence of the *razana* and in their ability to grant both healing and sickness. Moreover, even those who had not received physical healing predominately believe in the power of the *razana* to both provide blessing, and when angered, bring about calamity.

PREVIOUS EXPOSURE TO SPIRIT POSSESSION

Question: Have you ever been possessed by the spirits? If so, please describe your experience.

Possession by a spiritual entity is widely accepted within the traditional Malagasy culture. Traditional Malagasy residents understand a host of spiritual beings to inhabit the world and at times to take up residence within humanity. Malagasy's who follow the traditional religions seek out spiritual-possession because they believe spirit-possession brings the capability to perform many tasks and provide an economic benefit. One of the most well-known forms of possession in Madagascar is *tromba* possession; however, the people also accept a host of other possible possessing entities. The first portion of this question sought to determine how many of the respondents considered themselves to have been possessed at some time during their pre-Christian state of being. Those interviewed demonstrate that the majority (54.7%) described themselves as being spirit-possessed by one or more entities at some time during their pre-Christian lives.

The second portion of the question seeks to understand the experiential aspects of possession. Of those reporting to have been possessed, they identify a wide range of spiritual agents (A complete listing of the known possessing entities can be found in the Malagasy worldview section of this book.) The majority of those reporting possession identified their possession as *tromba* possession. However, many other spirits were also identified. Some of those questioned reported multiple occurrences of possession. One man explains how he became possessed at an early age:

> There was an *angabe* dwelling within me. Through it, I could relate directly to the *razana*. My father put this spirit within me when I was very young. I also had other spirits dwelling

within me, the spirits of *bazaha, antakarana,* and *betsimisaraka.*[14]

A large number of people reported experiencing possession from early childhood. However, others describe an adult onset of possession. One of the most feared forms of possession is *zavarindrano* possession. *Zavarindrano* are water spirits (mermaids) that bring considerable confusion and sickness upon their hosts. Only two of those questioned reported this type of possession, and their stories are some of the most dramatic of the stories found in this book. Therefore, an extended account of one individual's story is presented below:

> Before becoming a Christian, I worshiped the *razana,* and I had a beast from the river that was inside of me called an *ambiroan-drano* (*zavarindrano* or mermaid). I had to talk to the beast every day and ask blessings from the *razana.* This beast was like my wife because she would not allow me to marry anyone. I did not approach any person to get the *ambiroan-drano.* I went and stood by the river at the end of the day when there was no sun. She called to me and took me into her home. Once there we called upon the *razana* and with them had a feast in her home. I loved the beast because of all of the blessings and wealth that she gave to me. We offered many sacrifices of cows and bulls as we called upon the *razana.* It was at this time that I consecrated all of the charms, branches, and leaves that this beast gave to me. My work was that of a fisherman. I threw my net into the river. During that time, I had a lot of financial difficulty. One day I caught a large number of fish, and I was astonished. I asked why I got these forty large fish. When I went to sleep in my house, a woman, the *ambiroan-drano,* came to me, and we made love. She said to me that she was the owner of the river and that she had given me the fish. It was after accepting to be her husband that my living standard became much better. I had difficulty calling this spirit a wife. I could touch her, I could kiss her, and I could talk to her. She had the appearance of a beautiful woman, like a person. No one could see her, but

---

[14] Interview S20M10.

only I could see her. However, one day the woman asked me for a terrible thing. She asked me to give to her the blood of the children of my sister. She wanted to drink their blood. When I reflected on that for a long time, she thought that I would divorce her. Then she took me by force into her home under the water, and we stayed there for one week. When I came back from her house, I called my family, and they forbade me to go to the water and fish anymore. They took me to the Lutheran Church, and the church preached to me the Gospel. One of my brother's children was a Lutheran. I told the Christians at his church my story, and they gave me a Bible and brought me every day to the *toby* to be exorcized. After one month, they brought me to church. When this occurred, my wife, the spirit, came to me and said, "I have come to bring you home." I saw her, and I told my family that she was there and my family called the *mpiandry* and they came and sent her away in the name of Jesus of Nazareth, and she disappeared. I could not see her anymore. It was then that I became Lutheran. The Lutheran faith sent her out of me for good, and she has never returned.[15]

This is just one example of how a possessed individual perceives their situation. Many other examples are reported in the in the coming chapters.

---

[15] Interview S30M10.

CHAPTER SIX

THE POSSESSED MIND

I was very sick because the bilo *tormented me. I became lame! I could not stand up and was required to lie down on the bed and not get up. I saw a man or thing that was very dark and he tormented me and threatened me.*

—An unnamed respondent

What goes on in the mind of the possessed? No one really knows. The best we can do is listen to the stories of those who have been demon-possessed and take them at face value. While we may naturally be suspicious of such stories, it is helpful to hear them from people we trust. There is a difference between the stories told by a dear friend or family member than someone we meet on the street. The stories presented in this book come from our brothers and sisters in the Christian Church, many of whom have become trusted leaders, including pastors and seminary professors.

This chapter contains two sections: the first describes how the converts were drawn to the Church, and the second section tells the stories of those who found release, forgiveness, and peace within the Church.

DEALING WITH SPIRITUAL CONCERNS: CONTEXT AND BACKGROUND

When the people were asked "What brought you to the church?" their resounding answer focused on two areas: personal evangelism and the

Malagasy Lutheran Church's ability to deal with the spiritual concerns of the people. These were the primary reasons given by the respondents for joining the Lutheran Church. The majority of those who became members of the Church had themselves, or someone close to them, experienced an illness prior to joining the Church. The primary illness identified was spiritual possession. Most Malagasy's report evangelistic contact with a member of the Lutheran Church due to the Malagasy Lutheran Church's well-designed lay outreach movement (the *Fifohazana* and *mpiandry*). Moreover, the Church has a reputation as being a place of spiritual healing. Therefore, many of those who join the Church reported being brought to the Lutheran Church by one of their friends, family, or *mpiandry*, during times of intense spiritual struggle and sickness.

PRE-CONVERTED STATE OF HEALTH

Question: How did you feel at that time in your life?

The responses suggest that many of the people had experiences with severe sickness. This question sought to determine if there were any connections between one's previous illnesses and one's pre-converted state.

The majority of the people questioned (53.2%) report experiencing an illness prior to becoming Christian. The next highest response (20.3%) were those who described someone close to them experiencing an illness. Therefore, more than 73 percent of those questioned identified a previous illness as a precursor to their attachment to the Lutheran Church.

Illness in the Malagasy worldview can range from physical, mental, or spiritual causes. Many times illness is understood in a holistic sense, i.e., related to the total being of the individual. Many of those describing themselves as experiencing an illness also identified themselves as previously possessed (43%). The following remarks demonstrate a relationship between spirit-possession and illness:

> My wife and I had a son. We received a large radio with a cassette. We used this to call upon the ancestors. Because I respected so much the *tromba*, he asked me to sacrifice my only child for him. I accepted, but my wife refused to put to death my child. Because my wife refused and hesitated, the *tromba* punished me. All of my body became covered with

wounds and boils filled with puss. I suffered so much that I finally called to the Lutheran *mpiandry* for help. Then a demon came to me. He was furious and said that he would kill me if I were to be separated from him. I told him that I was suffering so much that I did not care if I died. Then the *mpiandry* exorcized me. I called on the name of Jesus, and all of my boils were healed. Then everything I had received from the devil disappeared, my wife, and even my child died.[1]

The *bilo* made me sick, and I would become unconscious. During this time, I would do things that I did not want to do.[2]

I was very sick because of the *tromba* that was inside of me. This is why I came to the Lutheran Church.[3]

I was sick because of the *kasoa* that was within me. It would make me cry out, and I could not control it.[4]

I was not sick, but my wife was tormented by the *tromba*. I sold much of my wealth to get her healed by the *ombiasy,* but she was not helped. I sold twenty cows and gave the *ombiasy* everything they wanted so that my wife could be healed, but she was not healed. Then some of the members of my family said I should go to church. The church told me there was exorcism, but I did not go at first. Some of my family were Catholic and said that I should not go.[5]

I was very sick because the *bilo* tormented me. I became lame! I could not stand up and was required to lie down on the bed and not get up. I saw a man or thing that was very dark, and he tormented me and threatened me.[6]

In the majority of the cases, this trend remains consistent. Those who identified illness within themselves, or someone close to them, believed those illnesses to be a result of spirit-possession.

---

[1] Interview S05M05.

[2] Interview S09M11.

[3] Interview S11M11.

[4] Interview S15M11.

[5] Interview S17M11.

[6] Interview S18M04.

EVANGELICAL CONNECTIONS

Question: Did you have any family or friends in the Malagasy Lutheran Church?

The purpose of this question was to determine the relationships those within the traditional religion shared with members of the Malagasy Lutheran Church prior to their conversion. Did traditional evangelism methods, such as the sharing of the Gospel by others, have a relationship to the respondents coming to church?

The majority of those questioned (56.2%) reported having family connections to the Lutheran Church. However, the result showed an inverse relationship when the respondents were limited to those who had reported an uncompromised allegiance to traditional religion. A cross tabulation of the data demonstrated the connection between those describing themselves as practitioners of the traditional religions (38 respondents) and their family connections within the Malagasy Lutheran Church.

Fifty percent of those questioned reported no family or friends attached to the Malagasy Lutheran Church prior to their conversion. The majority of those questioned reported an antagonistic relationship with Christianity. One man remarked:

> When I was an *ombiasy,* the Christian religion was my enemy, and Lutheran Christians even came to me to look for charms and talisman for their own use. Many times I would send demons to attack the Christians who had a weak faith. Some Christians became our friends and others did not. Those who did not become our friends had something "white" within their hearts. There were some who came and preached the Gospel to me, but I refused their Gospel. The day of my healing became a great day for me, and everyone heard about it. I was then educated in the Holy Scriptures and was baptized. I asked the pastor to change my name, so they changed my name from "Soft" to *Kalb.* I was then commissioned as a *mpiandry* and later became a pastor.[7]

This type of response was typical of many of those without previous attachments to the Lutheran Church.

---

[7] Interview S05M05.

One of the women interviewed stated:

> At that time, it was me and my boss that did the work of the *ombiasy*. I had no family with me, but I had the charms and the cows that stayed with me. The Christians were *taboo* for me so I ran away from them and I avoided all contact with the Christians.[8]

The next response speaks of a fear held for the Lutheran Church and its practice of exorcism:

> I did not have any Christians in my family. My family considered Christians to be our enemies, especially the Lutheran Church, because we believed that exorcism would take away the power of our charms and talisman.[9]

While 50 percent of those questioned had no prior attachment through family or otherwise to the Lutheran Church, those who did report an attachment considered it to be extremely limited, i.e., a distant relative was a member of the church, but the respondents identified no interaction with the church. Many of the respondents reported their initial contact to the church through family or other relationships. The following responses are typical of this group:

> When I decided to go to church, I approached a girl who was my friend. She was a member of the Malagasy Lutheran Church. She advised me and taught me many things about the Christian religion. She also taught me that worshiping the dead was the wrong way.[10]

> My first and second daughters became married to people in the Lutheran Church. It was in the house of my first daughter that I became a Christian.[11]

> One of my brother's children was a Lutheran. I told the Christians at his church my story, and they gave me a Bible and brought me every day to the *toby* to be exorcized.[12]

---

[8] Interview S22F20.

[9] Interview S52F16.

[10] Interview S12F05.

[11] Interview S26F05.

[12] Interview S29M05.

Other respondents reported members of the church evangelizing them in times of need. The next two responses describe these experiences:

> The priest from the Roman Catholic Church came to me many times, but he could do nothing to help me. The Lutheran pastor came to me and relieved me of the *tromba* spirit that tormented me. It was then that I became attached to the Lutheran Church.[13]

> The Lutheran Church visited me in prison. They brought me back to the Lutheran Church. The chief of the prison was a *Mpiandry*. He received me as a son.[14]

These answers signify that the Malagasy Lutheran Church has a strong evangelism program that reaches many within the community. However, the research also suggests that an equal number of pre-converted Malagasies had no relationship with any representative of the Lutheran Church prior to conversion.

INITIAL INTEREST IN THE CHURCH

Question: When did you first consider coming to the Lutheran Church? Describe what you were experiencing.

This question has two parts. The first part seeks to determine which factors attracted the respondents to the Lutheran Church. The second part of the question seeks to understand the experience surrounding that attraction.

The data suggests that personal evangelism (37.5%), that is, members of the church speaking to people about their faith and bringing friends and family to church, is the single primary reason respondents reported coming to the Lutheran Church. However, when the questions related to personal spiritual struggles and family struggle combined (42.2%), the emphasis switches to the Lutheran Church's ability to address the spiritual problems of the respondents as the greatest reason for attachment to the church.

The peoples' experiences are broad in scope. Therefore, this section provides a range of responses. The answers personal

---

[13] Interview S37M00.

[14] Interview S57M06.

evangelism (37.5%) and help with problems of a spiritual nature (42.4%) tend to be the primary reasons reported for seeking out the Lutheran Church.

Personal Evangelism

Many of those seeking out membership in the Malagasy Lutheran Church identify personal evangelism as their primary connection with the church. The responses that follow are representative of the typical comment offered.

> I do not remember the date when I became a Christian, but the youth were the ones who brought me to the church to see them perform. Finally, one day I was baptized.[15]

> One day in 2005, some Christians traveled to a church, which they did every two months. They would pass by the village and sing hymn 409[16] to us as they passed. The song touched my ears and my heart. I asked the Christians to come into my house. The Christians were afraid because I was the one who helped the *maha-lonaky* in the village, but they came into our house. We asked them to sing, and I loved what they sung.[17]

> In 2002, the Lutheran catechist came to preach in our house. He preached Mark 10:9. At the time, we were about to divide our home because we were about to divorce.[18]

---

[15] Interview S33M20.

[16] Included is the translation of hymn 409. It is dialogue between God, our Father, calling His children to come back to Him, and His children accepting the call. This hymn is often sung during a *Fifohazana* service. It is a call for repentance from ancestor worship habits. It shows also the loving and forgiving heart God.

1. "O children who are gone astray, come back!" your Father calls you; We will respond freely without any constraint. "Here we are. We confess that we are not good, and we are wounded by the enemy; Heal us because our way of living is corrupted." 2. "Oh, we have sinned and deserved to die and to be condemned forever! Our ancestors have worshiped the dead and we have followed them. O Father look at us and save us so that we may become Your children. We, who now bow down our head before You." 3. "I will heal your going astray O my children! I will not also make my face sad (*ampanjomboniko*) for you." That what we want to hear in our heart is that You are our Father who comforts Your people."

[17] Interview S62M10.

[18] Interview S67F16.

I will never forget the day when the *mpiandry* came and preached to me. They preached that all things are vanity and vain. The only thing of value is Jesus. Everything else can only lead to destruction, but Jesus has wealth. He who believes in Jesus receives all things freely. When I heard this, I threw away all of my charms and became a Lutheran, and I was baptized.[19]

In 1986, I became a Lutheran. The Lutherans came to my house one day. They came to pray for me and preach the word of God to me. They told me that God loved sinners.[20]

When my house was burned down, everyone from the village came to present their condolences to me, but when the Christians came they gave to us many things, like clothes, food, and money, but they also preached to us the Gospel. I remember very well the verse they brought to me, Matthew 11:28. Through their preaching, I trusted in Jesus and decided to become a Lutheran Christian.[21]

These responses provide an insight into the evangelism methods of the Malagasy Lutheran Church. The methods described are holistic in nature; they range from individual Christians speaking to their neighbors about the hope they have in Jesus, to mercy care, which seeks to address the problems and needs of the society. The majority of those who sought out the Lutheran Church did so because of the love they perceived extended to them by the actions of the Church and its Lord, Jesus Christ.

Problems of a Spiritual Nature

The majority of those who sought out membership in the Malagasy Lutheran Church (42.4%) identified spiritual problems and the desire for release as the connection point they sought with the church. The responses that follow are representative of the typical responses offered.

---

[19] Interview S22F20.

[20] Interview S20M10.

[21] Interview S19M21.

These *tromba* tormented me so much that during the fifteen days of torment I was unconscious, but I felt pain everywhere because the *tromba* threw me on the ground many times. After that, my daughter brought some of the *mpiandry* from the church into the house and they exorcized me and the house three times per day. After fifteen days, I was healed and felt lighter and became a Lutheran.[22]

In 1998, there was a *Fifohazana* in *Ambohimahasoa* (that is the Southern part of Madagascar). Many people were healed, and my child brought me there to get a solution. The glory of God was manifest, and I was healed. I recovered my mind and decided to begin confirmation class at the *toby*.[23]

Every day my sickness tormented me, and everyone in the house was unhappy because they stayed with me. The evangelist asked my father to take me to his home. After three days of exorcism my life became as a light. It was then that I decided to become a Lutheran.[24]

I was mentally ill and sought out many people for help; finally, someone brought me to the *Fifohazana* for an exorcism. After that, I was brought to the *toby* and stayed there. Every day I went through exorcism, and heard the preaching and finally I was healed. After being healed, I went through the training to be baptized.[25]

In 1985, when I could not be healed by my charms, my skin became white (leprosy). Therefore, I went to the Lutheran church because as a Catholic, there was no exorcism in the Roman Catholic Church.[26]

I did not think about becoming Lutheran, but when I saw that my wife was healed I decided to become a Lutheran.[27]

---

[22] Interview S26F05.

[23] Interview S30M10.

[24] Interview S51F21.

[25] Interview S52F16.

[26] Interview S08M11.

[27] Interview S01M11.

17. Shepherds praying for sick children at a *Fifohazana* service.

In each of these cases, as well as many others of those interviewed, personal healing of one's self or of one's family members was the deciding factor that brought people to the Lutheran Church. Throughout the island, the recognition of the exorcism as found in the Malagasy Lutheran Church motivates people to seek out help and the deliverance from the demonic possession through the church. People recognize that the Church has an answer for the problems they face and will provide both help and assistance to those in need.

DRAMATIC CONVERSIONS

Question: When did you become a Christian? Please tell us about that experience. Where were you (church, home, street, *toby*)?

For many of us who have grown up in the church, this would be a difficult question to answer. Many would point to their Baptism as infants; however, the situation in Madagascar is very different. While most of the growth in the Western Church occurs through the transfer of memberships or the Baptism of children born into Christian families, this is not the case in Madagascar. Most of their growth comes from conversion growth: peoples coming from the traditional religions after hearing the Gospel message through the conduit of exorcism. The majority of those interviewed (35.9%) described the church as the location of their conversion. However, the *toby* (a camp of healing) was the second most significant location identified by the respondents.

Those who described themselves as previously possessed overwhelmingly identified the *toby* as the central location of their conversion (37%) with the next highest response identified as "unspecified" (22.9%). The church (20%) and the personal residence (17%) were respectively in the third and fourth locations. The research demonstrates the majority of those who experienced a conversion (77%) did so outside of the church building. Research shows that the *mpiandry* of the *Fifohazana* movement conduct their operations primarily in the field, that is, where the people live and work. Moreover, the work of conversion carried out in the field is primarily connected to exorcism.

18. This one example of a Lutheran *toby* complete
with hospital and chapel, near Antananarivo, Madagascar.

The Phenomena of Exorcism and Conversion—Stories of Struggle

When the demons saw that I wanted to be Christian they appeared to me with knives and spears and wanted to kill me. One day they wanted to throw me into the fire. They frightened me and that fear was very heavy upon me.

—A recent convert to Christianity

This section gets to the heart of the experiences of exorcism and conversion found in the Malagasy Lutheran Church. The people were asked to describe in detail the experiences they had during their conversions.

The findings demonstrate that in their pre-converted state, the majority of the people described their lives as battlefields in which they fought against the *taboos* of the *razana* and the oppression of the spirits that possessed them. The next highest response described was an inward battle with their personal sin. Repeatedly, one, if not both, of these experiences were described. As to conversion, many of the people questioned described the release they experienced through exorcism. Once the spirits left them, they described the feeling of either repentance or great sorrow over their previous sins against Jesus. However, the overwhelming response of those who described their conversions did so in terms of peace, freedom, and release. Release from the torment of their personal sins as well as release from the bondage of the *razana*, *ombiasy*, and other spiritual forces that had previously oppressed them.

Pre-Conversion Experiences

Question: What did you experience before your conversion?

The purpose of this question was to determine what experiences the respondents had prior to conversion. The research demonstrated that the majority of the people (40.6%) described their pre-converted state as one of struggle with the spirits. The spirits described were those generally accepted by the traditional culture (*tromba, lolo, bilo,* etc.). The following comments represent the experience expressed by the majority of individuals:

Before I was converted to Christianity, the devils had power over me. I followed much of what they told me to do. When the demons saw that I wanted to be Christian they appeared to me with knives and spears and wanted to kill me. One day they wanted to throw me into the fire. They frightened me, and that fear was very heavy upon me. However, I did not listen to their threats, but I decided to become a Christian.[28]

Before my conversion, I saw a person appear before me, and I would talk to him, but no one else could see him. When the *tromba* wanted to possess me they would appear as huge black things that came and covered me, all of my body was under their possession.[29]

Before my conversion, my life with Satan was bad. I had much suffering and poverty. I had a sickness of mind that was difficult to heal.[30]

Before my conversion, I saw in my dreams many people who wanted to kill me. This happened when I did not yet go to church. I would go to the *ombiasy* to have my dreams stop. However, the *ombiasy* could not help.[31]

This trend continues amongst the majority of individuals questioned. Each of them describes a similar experience that focuses upon a spiritual phenomenon, i.e., a demonic entity.

The second largest group of respondents identified their conversion in terms of an enlightened experience of repentance. Over 20 percent (21.9%) of those interviewed described their pre-converted state as an experience of personal struggle over sin. The following represent the majority of experiences:

Before I was converted, I had an internal fight within me between becoming Christian and being the head of the family who is the keeper of the tradition (family priest). I had many responsibilities as head of the family; because of this there was an internal fight inside of me. In addition, my children

---

[28] Interview S25F05.

[29] Interview S27F10.

[30] Interview S35F06.

[31] Interview S53F21.

were pagan and did not want me to become Christian for fear of losing them.[32]

Because I practiced the way of getting many cows (sacrifice to the *razana*), there were spirits of the dead within me. When I heard the call of the Holy Spirit to become a Christian an eternal fight occurred within me. Sometimes the spirits of the dead would appear to me and threaten to kill me. They would also threaten me through blackmails and forced me to return to the *ombiasy* and practice my former job, but I did not listen to them. I trusted in God.[33]

What I felt before my conversion was the lack of peace of mind and the lack of sleep.[34]

In each of these cases, the people described some form of internal conflict or struggle prior to conversion. Many of the respondents continued to express similar experiences when answering the following question.

THE RELATIONSHIP BETWEEN CONVERSION AND EXORCISM

Question: What did you experience at the time of your conversion?

The purpose of this question was to discover what experiences those who converted to Christianity experienced during their conversion. The majority of the respondents fell within two categories of experience: they either described a feeling of deep repentance (33.3%) or a feeling of extraordinary peace and freedom (31.7%). The following are responses that are typical to the first group followed by the responses of the latter.

Post Conversion Experiences of Repentance

When I became a Christian I then saw how bad all the things I had done were, and I felt ashamed because of all of the bad things I did in the community. However, when I became converted, I got a new heart and was a great sign to all of the

---

[32] Interview S18M04.

[33] Interview S23M04.

[34] Interview S67F16.

people. The power of Jesus has freed me and no one can enslave me again.[35]

There were not many good things in my life before my conversion, but through the problems I faced I learned that Jesus loved me. He stretched out His hands with love to receive me. He makes my spirit alive, and His grace, which is new every day, protects and forgives me.[36]

Before I was sick. I hated the Christians and the Christian religion. I loved to go to festivals and drink alcohol. I also loved to find women to take for myself. I went to the Saturday market. This means to look for a woman for sexual purposes. After my conversion, I loved the Christian life. What I loved before I now hate, and what I hated before I love now. I cannot wait for Sunday so that I can go to church and listen to the preaching.[37]

After my conversion, I understood that all good things come from God. Rather than thinking I am better than other people are, now I know I am nothing apart from Jesus. Now I have good relations with other people because I began to learn how to love and care for others. I began to preach to others that there are no blessings from the *razana*. Only Jesus can bless you and give to you all the grace you need . . .[38]

After my conversion, I was ashamed of what I did. Now I am changed, and I have a joy because I am changed. I no longer worship the charms. I rely on the power of God now.[39]

Repentance is always a work of God upon the heart of man; the Holy Spirit Himself works this repentance, which can be considered in two parts. One part is noted in the above interviews. As Holy Scripture (Acts 11:18) teaches, a genuine sorrow over sins is created through the knowledge of the individual's sins. Also the Holy Spirit, through the forgiveness of sins, creates faith that believes the

---

[35] Interview S05M05.

[36] Interview S13F05.

[37] Interview S19M21.

[38] Interview S36F05.

[39] Interview S54M11.

conscience has peace and freedom from terrors and guilt.[40] Therefore, we should expect stories of this nature to be prevalent in the lives of those freed from the darkness and brought into the light. The next section provides the personal stories of those who continue to live this life of peace and forgiveness.

Post Conversion Experiences of Peace and Freedom

> I was very violent and could not show mercy to anyone. The *angabe* controlled me and made me do many terrible things. Everyone was afraid of me and all of the spirits of the *razana* who dwelt within me. Few were those who could compete with me. I could heal everyone, and I hated the Lutheran Church. I experienced a great release and happiness following my conversion. I now have a good relationship with everyone around me. The constant battle that was taking place within me ceased when the *angabe* departed from me. Even though people teased me about my former conduct, I did not get angry with them, but only thanked Jesus for setting me free.[41]

> Many were the difficulties in my life. Many times the *tromba* would make me sleep outside of my house, at the river, or in the forest. Many foods were taboo for me. I could not eat meats such as pork, eel, porcupine, bats, shrimps, crabs, and certain leaves. I was not permitted to wear cloths with more than one color. In brief, my life was very narrow. When I became Christian, I found out that the faith of my children was good, and that faith liberated me from many chains. I now know that it was the work of the darkness that I followed before, but now I follow Jesus who has liberated us from many things.[42]

> I was always in anguish during my life and I was afraid. I never got the things I wanted in my life. The *tromba* did not allow me to eat most foods: no pork, no beef, no chicken wings, or greens. After my conversion, I received freedom. I am not afraid. I have no anguish. I have a love for the people

---

[40] See AC XII.

[41] Interview S20M10.

[42] Interview S27F10.

around me. I was no longer in difficulty. The spirits of the dead no longer came to me. When they came to me I prayed and they disappeared.[43]

Before my conversion, I was in great difficulty because I had to choose only the food the *tromba* would allow. I could not eat pork, duck, chicken, shrimp, and greens. Even the time to come and go from our home was chosen by the *tromba*. I was very thin because my life was terrible.[44]

The worship of the *razana* brought much suffering to our life because we always depended upon them for everything. We had to make vows and bring sacrifices to satisfy them. The most difficult was the keeping of the taboos. When I came to the Lutheran Church, I found happiness because Jesus Christ liberated me from the taboos. Now my life is good because I no longer have fear in our life.[45]

Repeatedly, the theme in these interviews is positive. The people do not claim that their lives are free from problems or worry. Many of them would describe their lives as being more difficult due to the social alienation and the loss of income they suffered following their conversions. However, in the midst of their earthly sufferings they have found freedom and peace through the Gospel. Many of them continue to experience suffering, starvation, sickness, and pain. They know that they will continue to face difficulties, just as their Lord did during His earthly ministry, but they can now face these difficulties with confidence in the resurrection and the continued presence of Jesus in their lives.

When the responses of these two groups are cross tabulated against their previous experiences with spirit-possession, a significant trend appears. Those who described themselves as previously possessed tend to describe their converted state as one of peace and freedom (43%) whereas those who answered negatively to the possession question (50%) tend to describe their converted status as one of deep repentance. While this is interesting, it should not surprise the reader. To most of those who were brought to faith in

---

[43] Interview S50F09.

[44] Interview S56M10.

[45] Interview S60M10.

society, repentance would likely be the primary emotion experienced. However, as our society continues to turn to the spirit-world and practices of divination and fortune-telling, it may see future generations also identifying with stories of bondage and terror. While at first this book may seem to be focused on faraway places it is my hope that as you continue to read through the remaining pages you will begin to see connections between the things described within this book and the lives of the people that surround you in your own neighborhoods.

POST-CONVERSION: EXPERIENCING LIFE FREE FROM THE BONDAGE OF THE DEVIL

Question: What were your experiences the moments directly following your conversion?

More than 70 percent (71.9%) of those questioned identified freedom, peace, and trust as outcomes of their conversion into the Christian faith. Conversion for them was release from the oppressive life under the law of the *razana* and the *ombiasy*. The following responses are representative of this group:

> Following my conversion, I gave Jesus my heart and my soul. The church burned the Muslim books and I became a servant of God. I felt that I was freed from slavery and the different various taboos that I used to live in. I was freed of anguish and sickness.[46]

> After my conversion, my life became very quiet and peaceful. No spirits came to frighten me anymore.[47]

> I ran away, and my charms were burned. When the *tromba* left me, I felt a change within me. Satan left me with anger, and I saw the hands of Jesus, who received me. When the *mpiandry* exorcized me, I saw the Holy Spirit come to me and take my hand. All of the chains that Satan had placed on my hands, feet, and throat—everything within me was loosened. Now I feel unchained. Before, I was chained to the

---

[46] Interview S01M11.

[47] Interview S21M11.

devil. Before I felt like I was always in a ditch, but now I always have happiness with Jesus.[48]

When I became Christian, I found out that the faith of my children was good, and that faith liberated me from many chains. I now know that it was the work of the darkness that I followed before, but now I follow Jesus, who has liberated me from many things.[49]

After my conversion, I received freedom. I am not afraid. I have no anguish, and I have a love for the people around me. I am no longer in difficulty. The spirits of the dead no longer came to me. When they came to me I prayed and they disappeared.[50]

When I came to the Lutheran Church, I found happiness because Jesus Christ liberated me from the taboos. Now we know that this is superstition. Now my life is good because we no longer have fear in our life.[51]

In each of these cases, as well as many others found in the research, the outcome expressed was one of freedom. Paul once wrote words to the Galatian Church that will be of help to us here. He writes, "For freedom Christ has set us free; stand firm therefore, and do not submit again to a yoke of slavery" (Galatians 5:1). To the Corinthians he writes, "Now the Lord is the Spirit, and where the Spirit of the Lord is, there is freedom" (2 Corinthians 3:17). Freedom is only found in Jesus and the places He has promised to be. Therefore, the next chapter focuses on the lives of these new converts who have been brought to faith within the communion of the Lutheran Church. What you are about to read will continue to astound you. If you have had reservations about these people and their experiences up to this point, the next chapter is sure to put your mind at ease in one sense, yet bring you discomfort in another. The discomfort you find may not be in what you learn about these Malagasy Christians, but what you notice missing from yourself.

---

[48] Interview S25F05.

[49] Interview S27F10.

[50] Interview S50F09.

[51] Interview S60M10.

CHAPTER SEVEN

STORIES OF LIFE IN THE CHURCH

The greatest thing the church did for me was exorcism. When I started to recover my health and became conscious, the church taught me and my parents the Scriptures and the Small Catechism. We did this every day. They also taught me how to pray. In 1980, we were baptized, me, my brother and my mother and father. I then studied and entered the seminary. I am now a pastor in the Lutheran Church.

—An unnamed respondent

Stories of conversion abound in all popular missiological writings, but the focus of this chapter is to follow-up on the lives of those who have gone from darkness to light. How many of those interviewed had returned to the ancestors or spirits for assistance? It is well-known that folk religion exists in all Christian denominations; would the Malagasy Lutheran Church show any exceptions to this rule? To determine the answer, the people were asked a basic question: "How has your life been affected by the Christian faith?"

This section is extremely significant because it demonstrates the effectiveness of the Malagasy Lutheran method of dealing with a populace who tend to follow false gods and have a history of returning to their previous religions during times of doubt or trouble. This question provides a glimpse into the daily life of the church—how Malagasy Christians understand their faith.

The Christian Life Post-Conversion

Thus far, the Malagasy Lutheran Church has been shown to be one that deals in power encounters and spiritual warfare. Moreover, we must admit that for many of us, this is certainly a foreign concept. Mainline Churches within the United States and Europe rarely discuss such themes as spiritual warfare and power encounters. Nevertheless, the people represented in this book continue to have a common response to questions about their lives. The gift of faith has brought about a new life of peace, and freedom to a people who once had only known darkness.

19. A typical Malagasy Lutheran church.

Yet, are these people actually Lutheran or have they just accepted the title brought by the early missionaries? The answer to this question must revolve around the doctrine of justification. What is their status before God? Can they do anything to earn God's favor and forgiveness? Can they provide sacrifices, as they were previously accustomed to doing, to appease God's anger and receive His blessings? How do they worship? Do they use a Lutheran Liturgy? Do they receive their catechesis through the instruction of Martin Luther's Small Catechism? This section of the book will answer these questions. Moreover, you as the reader will be surprised when you read the story of these new Lutheran Christians that have been brought to faith through the Word and Sacrament. Indeed, they will use all of the Lutheran terminology.

These far away people's church body contains more than twice the number of Lutherans found in The Lutheran Church—Missouri Synod, understand more than most the worldly benefit of Jesus and His cross. As you will read, they speak in terms of declarative righteousness, and they recognize that they no longer need to work for salvation and peace; it is already theirs in Jesus. For these people, the church has taken the place of their extended family. Previously, spiritual allegiance with the Malagasy family of spirits and ancestors was demanded. Now the new family of the church brings a life of freedom, release, and hope. However, currently the only spiritual allegiances identified by the respondents are to Jesus. While some identified the pastors as helpers in this regard, they only functioned in an assisting role. In some ways, in the minds of various people, the pastors took the position once held by the *ombiasy*. However, unlike in their traditional religion, the pastor is not an intermediary, but only a servant. The pastor's purpose is to preach, teach, and preside over the sacraments of the church. The people overwhelmingly acknowledged their reception of the Holy Word and Holy Sacraments as the means they employed in overcoming their current problems. Throughout the interviews, there was no syncretism or the mixing of traditional religions with the Christian faith acknowledged by any of the respondents. This is interesting because the Malagasy people have a strong history of syncretistic worship.[1] The remainder of this

---

[1] Previous responses have demonstrated that the majority of the respondents were syncretistic prior to their conversion and membership in the Malagasy Lutheran

chapter tells the story of the lives of the people now that they are members of the church.

20. Recent converts studying the Bible and Luther's Small Catechism.

A NEW LIFE IN THE PROTECTION OF MOTHER CHURCH

Question: What is the difference in your life now, since you left your previous religion (Animism)?

All of us change as we age. Circumstances and events in life form and mold how we view the world, God, and our connection to others. In this section, we will discover how the Christian faith has formed and molded these Christian brothers and sisters who once worshiped false gods and ultimately the devil.

The interviews provide compelling depictions of what is occurring in the Malagasy Church. The majority of those questioned described their life in the church in terms of freedom (28.6%) and peace (34.9%). This is consistent with the remarks heard immediately following their stories of exorcism and conversion. Some of those interviewed identified other areas of importance. The next highest responses were either identification with the *mpiandry* movement (12.7%) or an unspecified experience (12.7%). To compare and contrast the post-conversion responses with the answers provided in

---

Church. Moreover, sources within the Malagasy Lutheran Church report syncretism to be a continual problem within their church body.

this section, the experiences of the people were analyzed in view of their new lives as Christians. How did they describe their new experiences compared to their earlier experiences? The following responses represent the two key experiences identified in the research groups: one, peace stemming from forgiveness; two, freedom from spiritual oppression.

Newfound Peace and Forgiveness

True forgiveness always brings peace. One can only have a true and lasting peace when one knows that there is finally freedom from oppression and condemnation. The title of this book came from this section. Here, you will read the words of freedom and release: "I am not afraid"! As you read through this section, listen carefully to the individual responses, for within them you will find a vast treasure waiting for you to uncover:

> There was a change in my life because I trusted in Jesus. I would like to remark that to hear and read the Word of God. I know that Jesus is with me in my life, and He answers prayers.[2]

> My life has changed drastically. No one is afraid of me anymore. I am now the president of my church. I live my life free from the taboos of the *razana*. I forgive those who are around me and I no longer have any hesitation, but I am always smiling and happy with people.[3]

> I have received a great change in my life. I am now a *mpiandry*, and there are no more demons assaulting me. I know that I was almost lost in hell when I was looking for the wealth of this world. I did not know that Jesus is the real wealth in heaven that will always remain.[4]

> The change I felt within me was one of liberation. I felt like I was rescued from a deep ditch were I was held captive. I

[2] Interview S06M05.

[3] Interview S20M10.

[4] Interview S23M04.

think about my family, and I am now trying to lead them to church. I believe that in Jesus there is eternal happiness.[5]

I am not afraid. Jesus is the real wealth. Jesus is the eternal happiness. These are words of joy and release. Release from the wages of sin and the powers of evil. However, the next section speaks even more clearly in terms of freedom. This freedom is not just from personal sin or oppression, but freedom from Satan and his kingdom.

A Freedom from Spiritual Oppression

The spirits are gone! Many of the people interviewed for this book had never known freedom before becoming Christians. They were born into families that worshiped the spirits and the ancestors. Many of them had been dedicated to these false deities when they were young. For many, spiritual oppression and demonic possession was all they had ever known. They had spent their lives in spiritual darkness and service to the spirits. As you read their responses, try to remember where they came from, what they endured, and the relevance of the new life they now have in Christ Jesus. Listen for the key themes of freedom and liberation:

> Now there is no illness at all; the devil has not returned. This was a big change in my life because I no longer followed the traditional religions. I put my life in the hands of Jesus and I never want to return to the traditional religions.[6]

> I am now completely free. Before the *bilo* forbade me to drink milk, to eat chicken, but now I can do these things.[7]

> Yes, I found a change in my life. I was now liberated from the power and taboos of the *razana*. There were no more taboos, especially in food.[8]

> There was a great change. Now I feel happy because now I do not have relations with the evil spirits.[9]

---

[5] Interview S28M05.

[6] Interview S08M11.

[7] Interview S10M04.

[8] Interview S15M11.

[9] Interview S65M04.

I am now liberated! I am now free! Thanks be to God through Jesus Christ my Lord! Yet, how does Jesus come to us? Where can we find Him? What is the function of the pastor and the church? The next section provides the answers to how and where these Malagasy Christians look for Jesus.

THE CHURCH: A PLACE OF FREEDOM, SPIRITUAL GUIDANCE, AND COMFORT

Question: To whom do you look for spiritual/physical help and comfort (witch doctors, ancestors, secular sources, priests, Christians, Jesus, etc.)? Do you continue to seek this help? What help do you experience?

This question relates to the previous chapter. However, whereas the previous chapter sought to determine the pre-converted spiritual associations of the respondents, this question seeks to determine the current spiritual associations of the respondents. The majority of people identified having an allegiance with Jesus (59.4%). The next two highest responses included the church (15.6%) and the pastor (10.9%); however, in each of the latter cases, after further questioning identified their association to the church and the pastor with their connection to Jesus. Therefore, more than 85 percent of the respondents (85.9%) claimed allegiance to Jesus.

How does this data compare with the initial data provided by the people prior to coming to church? There is a significant difference between the two. The traditional religion of animism focused on an intermediary; therefore, in the pre-converted state the majority of the people (37.5%) identified the local diviner *(ombiasy)* as the primary focus of allegiance. However, following their conversion into the Christianity the majority now described a direct allegiance with Jesus without the necessity of a mediator.

The following responses are typical of the majorities experience in the church:

Today, when something difficult comes to my life I do not look for someone or something else to help me. I feel that Jesus has helped me a lot. And the other Christians and the pastor comfort and encourage me to do that.[10]

---

[10] Interview S01M11.

I approach Jesus to help me in my life. I go to Him now rather than to the devil. He has given me my Baptism, and He has restored my health.[11]

I come to Jesus to help me in my life. The greatest gift I have received is the liberation from my job as *ombiasy* and all of the taboos that controlled my life.[12]

I approach the pastor when I have difficult times and he speaks to me the Holy Scriptures. Finally, the pastor worked with me and taught me how to read the Scriptures so that I can now read them to myself and others.[13]

We no longer go to the *ombiasy* anymore but now only to Jesus. I pray to Jesus every day to save the rest of my family who are pagan. I ask the pastor and the church to help pray for my family.[14]

Jesus, Jesus, only Jesus—this is the common response of the people. However, these people portray their attachment to Jesus in Lutheran terminology: Holy Baptism, the Holy Scriptures, and Holy Communion—these are the places where Jesus is to be found. While none of the responses provided here mentioned Holy Communion, the prominence of this Sacrament will be clear in the coming responses.

LOOKING FOR SYNCRETISM

Question: What, if any, experience do you continue to have with the spirits?

While many religious bodies claim to have gained converts from the animistic religions, repeatedly a high level of syncretism remains. This question seeks to determine what if any level of syncretism exists amongst the Lutherans interviewed. The results are encouraging. None of the people questioned openly identified themselves as continuing an association with the traditional religions (syncretism). In almost every case, there is a clear disassociation with

---

[11] Interview S08M11.

[12] Interview S15M11.

[13] Interview S20M10.

[14] Interview S34F04.

both the ancestors (*razana*) and the diviners (*ombiasy*) of the traditional religions. However, some of the respondents reported early temptations in this direction. One person stated:

> Sometimes I wanted to return to my previous life because then I was wealthy but the servant of God came to help me and these desires became reduced. Now I no longer desire to return. I pray in the name of Jesus my Lord.[15]

Compelling is the fact that often separation from the traditional beliefs comes at a great cost in terms of worldly wealth and relationships. Departure from the traditional beliefs normally results in excommunication from the traditional Malagasy family unit. In order to maintain membership within the family it is mandatory to participate in the religious rites of the tomb, which includes both financing and participating in the rituals of the *famadihana.* This is a significant obstacle to the newly converted, yet all of the respondents reported overcoming this obstacle. How was it overcome? Proper catechesis and participation within the liturgical life of the Church (Divine Service) provides the answer as demonstrated in the next section.

ECCLESIAL ACTIVITIES AND CATECHESIS

Question: How does the church help you overcome your problems?

All these interviewed reported the church as their new family. The church is the place in which Jesus delivers His gifts of Word and Sacrament. The people rely upon one another and the pastor as the family of God. The majority of those questioned (51.6%) reported Word and Sacrament as the primary gifts they receive from the church.[16] This demonstrates the distinct Lutheran identity of these Christian converts. Moreover, the respondents described themselves

---

[15] Interview S60M10.

[16] "The foundation of the healing ministry is the healing power of the Gospel . . . The forgiveness of sins by God is the most potent healing medication known to humankind. When a person is forgiven, the consequences touch not only the life of the spirit but the emotions and physical processes as well." Garth D. Ludwig, *Order Restored: A Biblical Interpretation of Health, Medicine, and Healing* (St. Louis: Concordia Academic Press, 1999), 205.

as a confessional church, specifically quoting the Small Catechism as the primary tool of their catechesis. The following responses demonstrate this point:

> The church always came to our home and asked us to go to church. They practiced exorcism every day in our home until we became free and were able to take the Lord's Supper. They taught us the Small Catechism and much about Jesus in our home. In 2003, we were commissioned as *mpiandry*.[17]

> The greatest thing the church did for me was exorcism. When I started to recover my health and became conscious, the church taught me and my parents the Scriptures and the Small Catechism. We did this every day. They also taught me how to pray. In 1980, we were baptized—me, my brother, and my mother and father. I then studied and entered the seminary. I am now a pastor.[18]

> During the time we stayed in the *toby* we received the exorcism and the laying on of hands. The pastor and the *mpiandry* took turns teaching us the Scriptures and the Small Catechism of the Lutheran Church. We now receive the Lord's Supper and continue to remain in the Lutheran Church.[19]

> When I learned how to read and write I was given a Bible by the church. I started to learn the Small Catechism and was baptized. My children and myself were all baptized. In 1991, I was married to another *mpiandry*, and she encouraged me to become a *mpiandry*. In 1996, I was commissioned as a *mpiandry*.[20]

While these responses demonstrate strong confessional adherents to the Lutheran Catechism, another principal theme is identified, namely exorcism. Exorcism is and remains a significant component of Malagasy Lutheran liturgical life.

---

[17] Interview S56M10.

[18] Interview S60M10.

[19] Interview S67F16.

[20] Interview S71M10.

PART ONE CONCLUSIONS

Part one of this book provided a comprehensive look into the lives of the Malagasy Lutheran Christians, specifically gaining an insider's perspective into what had occurred in the events surrounding their conversion. While their responses may be difficult for western minds to comprehend, they remain the experiences of these faithful Christians. Many, if not most, of those who read this book will not understand the tremendous fear and oppression these people have reported, but for them, it was real and traumatic. The majority of those questioned reported being demonically possessed before being brought to Jesus. Following their conversion into the Christian faith the overwhelming number of respondents described their lives in terms of peace and release from the oppression of the spirits or their representatives (*ombiasy*). Moreover, most of the respondents have now become the new religious leaders of the *Fifohazana* movement and have advanced into high ranks within the synodical structure of the Malagasy Lutheran Church.

21. Pastors of the Lutheran Church of Madagascar gathered at the historic Farihimena *toby* for the yearly *Fifohazana* meeting.

Sacramental theology also remains a high priority among the respondents. The majority specifically identified the hearing of the Holy Word and the reception of the Holy Sacraments as the means by which they are strengthened and protected in their Christian life. This is most likely due to the high regard the Malagasy Lutheran Church places on teaching (catechesis). A number of the people mentioned the catechesis they had received after coming to the church.[21] In each case, they described learning Martin Luther's Small Catechism and the Holy Scriptures. The liturgy and the hymns were also required memorization for all catechumens. As a result of both their new lives of freedom, peace, and their confessional subscription and scriptural knowledge, none of the respondents reported any form of syncretism or lapses into their previous religious allegiances. Here we see the promises of Jesus within the lives of these new Christians, "So if the Son sets you free, you will be free indeed" (John 8:36).

---

[21] Randrianasolo describes a typical catechism class taught in the Malagasy Lutheran Church. He writes, "Baptism was taught to the members of the confirmation class. Baptism was set over against ancestor worship and its corollaries. The teaching of the sacrament of the Lord's Supper followed the same line. Baptism and the Lord's Supper were closely delivered to the Confirmation class. Baptism was the entry door to salvation. It was also the entry door to membership of the church. It was also the step leading to the Lord's Table. Baptism and the Lord's Supper fed one another." Joseph Randrianasolo, *Camp Of Joy Lutheran Church: Where Is Your Child?* diss., Concordia Theological Seminary, 2009, 28.

PART TWO

EXORCISM – TEACHING FROM SCRIPTURE AND THE LIFE OF THE CHURCH

CHAPTER EIGHT

CHRIST BOUND SATAN
SO THAT WE MAY BE FREE

When Satan comes upon you at night, you shall say to him:
Who are you, oh offspring of man and of the seed of holy
ones? Your face is a face of delusion, and your horns of
illusion. You are darkness and not light, injustice and not
justice . . .

—An apocryphal psalm ascribed to King Solomon

If you have reached this part of the book, it should be clear to you that
the Malagasy Lutherans accept the biblical reality of demons and
exorcism. This chapter will focus on two questions. First, do demons
exist and can they be cast out through exorcism? Second, what was
the practice of exorcism during Jesus' ministry and in the Early
Church? We will answer these questions by reviewing the New
Testament texts that deal with demons and exorcism. These texts will
include those that describe the exorcism practices of Jesus and the
authority and command given to the early Christians to follow His
example.

By the time of Jesus, the Jews had established their own system
of exorcism, "complete with apparatus of formulae and measures that
were supposed to be effective against demons."[1] The Dead Sea
Scrolls help to shed some light on these early Jewish exorcisms.

---

[1] Gerhard Kittel, Geoffrey William Bromiley, and Gerhard Friedrich, *Theological
Dictionary of the New Testament*, vol. 1 (Grand Rapids: Eerdmans, 1964), 528.

Scroll 11Q11 is an apocryphal psalm ascribed to King Solomon.[2] This ancient fragment describes an incantation used when performing an exorcism. Notice the importance given to the use of the name of Yahweh:

> An incantation in the name of YAHW[H]. Invoke at an[y] time the heave[ns.] [When] he comes upon you at nig[ht,] you shall [s]ay to him: Who are you, [oh offspring of] man and of the seed of ho[ly] ones? Your face is a face of [delus]ion, and your horns of illu[si]on. You are darkness and not light, [injus]tice and not justice, [. . .] the chief of the army. YHWH [will bring] you down [to the] deepest [Sheo]l, [he will shut] the two bronze [ga]tes through [which n]o light [penetrates.] [On you shall] not [shine the] sun, whi[ch rises] [upon the] just man [. . .] You shall say [. . .] [. . . the ju]st man, to go [. . .] a de[mon] mistreats him. [. . .] [. . . tr]uth from . . . [. . . because jus]tice is with him [. . .] [. . .] . . . [. . .][3]

While there is no evidence of the effectiveness of this form of exorcism, it does provide insight into one of the Jewish rites. Indeed, Jesus implies that such Jewish exorcisms were, in fact, effective.[4] However, Jesus is capable of casting out the demons with a simple command and completely ignores Jewish apparatus.[5] He is the Living Word of God. His word is a performative word.[6] What He speaks must occur. Therefore, before Jesus the demons are helpless to do anything other than what He commands. Moreover, Jesus' exorcisms, as well as those of His followers, have a particular significance—they are pointing to the kingdom of God that has now come amongst the people. The restoration has begun. Jesus is demonstrating His omnipotent power over what Satan had considered his own personal domain.[7] Each time Jesus casts out demons, or brings healing to the

---

[2] Eric Sorensen, *Possession and Exorcism in the New Testament and Early Christianity* (Tübingen: Mohr Siebeck, 2002), 53.

[3] 11Q11 Col. V. See Sorensen, *Possession and Exorcism*, 69.

[4] Matthew 12:27; Luke 11:19.

[5] Kittel, *Theological Dictionary of the New Testament*, 528.

[6] R. C. H. Lenski, *The Interpretation of St. Luke's Gospel* (Columbus: Wartburg Press, 1946), 261.

[7] Lenski, *The Interpretation of St. Luke's Gospel*, 261.

afflicted, Satan's power is defeated.[8] Through the exorcisms recorded in the New Testament, Jesus is "driving back the effects of sin."[9] Jesus is the Son of the Most High God while Satan and his demons are weak and pitiful foes. There is no room for dualism in God's Kingdom.[10] There is one true power, namely, the triune God. If Satan possesses any power at all, it is only that which God has allowed him to exercise. However, the time has come for the binding of the "Strong Man."[11] Jesus is claiming what is His own as He takes back that which is rightfully His, that is, fallen humanity. He does this as He takes the sins of the world onto Himself and carries them to a cross.[12]

THE ULTIMATE AUTHORITY OF JESUS

Scripture demonstrates the ultimate authority of Jesus in the vocabulary it uses. For this reason, it is necessary to become acquainted with a series of words that relate to the topic of exorcism. Some of the Greek words in this section have a more technical use. Moreover, many of the words associated with exorcism are found in a verbal form and can be used in various contexts, many of which are outside the framework of exorcism. The purpose of this section is to provide the reader with the specific vocabulary Jesus used concerning exorcism by giving a short etymology of the words along with their frequency of use.

The first and most significant word associated with exorcism is *ekballō*. This Greek word is usually translated "cast out." However, *ekballō* can have at least five meanings, which include; (a) throw out (b) drive out, send out, (d) lead out, (e) exorcise, or (f) cause to be.[13]

---

[8] Jeffrey A. Gibbs, *Matthew 1:1–11:1*. Concordia Commentary. (St. Louis: Concordia, 2006), 224.

[9] Gibbs, *Matthew 1:1–11:1*, 224.

[10] Paul Tillich takes up the question of dualism in his Systematic Theology. Paul Tillich, *Systematic Theology: 1, Reason and Revelation Being and God* (Chicago: University of Chicago Press, 1973), 225.

[11] Matthew 12:29; Mark 3:27; Luke 11:21.

[12] Arthur A. Just Jr., *Luke 1:1–9:50*. Concordia Commentary. (St. Louis: Concordia, 1996), 200.

[13] Bible Works, computer software, Friberg Lexicon, version 4.0 (Norfolk: Bible Works, 2007).

Ekballō is a common word in the Greek New Testament and occurs eighty-one times, yet because of its various definitions, many of its occurrences extend into areas unrelated to demons or exorcism. In its various forms, the word *ekballō* occurs twenty-five times in Matthew's Gospel,[14] eighteen times in Mark's Gospel,[15] seventeen times in Luke's Gospel,[16] six times in John's Gospel,[17] and five times in the Book of Acts.[18] Matthew uses the word *ekballō* twelve times in his Gospel, referring to casting out a demonic entity.[19] Mark uses the word ten times in the context of exorcism.[20] Luke uses it eight times. However, none of Luke's writings uses the word in an exorcistic context.[21] John's Gospel only uses it in the context once.[22] While commonly the word is used to describe the action of an exorcism, Jesus and His disciples also use additional commands, which include *exerchomai*, *epitimaō*, *hypagō*, and *paragnellō*.

The Greek word *exerchomai* can mean to (a) go out or (b) pass away.[23] It occurs 218 times (in its various forms) in the New Testament with six of its occurrence relate to exorcism.[24] Generally, when related to exorcism the word is used as an imperative, "come out."[25] However, on two occasions Luke records it as an infinitive. Jesus commands the demons to come out of their hosts—there is no negotiation, the command is given, and the demons obey.

---

[14] Matthew 7:4; 7:5; 7:22; 8:12; 8:16; 8:31; 9:25; 9:33; 9:34; 9:38; 10:1; 10:8; 12:20; 12:24; 12:26; 12:27; 12:28; 12:35; 13:52; 15:17; 17:19; 21:12; 21:39; 22:13; 25:30.

[15] Mark 1:12; 1:34; 1:39; 1:43; 3:15; 3:22; 3:23; 5:40; 6:13; 7:26; 9:18; 9:28; 9:38; 9:47; 11:15; 12:8; 16:9; 16:17.

[16] Luke 4:29; 6:22; 6:42; 9:40; 9:49; 10:2; 10:35; 11:14; 11:15; 11:18; 11:19; 11:20; 13:28; 13:32; 19:45; 20:12; 20:15.

[17] John 2:15; 6:37; 9:34; 9:35; 10:4; 12:31.

[18] Acts 7:58; 9:40; 13:50; 16:37; 27:38.

[19] Matthew 7:22; 8:16; 8:31; 9:33; 9:34; 10:1; 10:8; 12:24; 12:26; 12:27; 12:28; 17:19.

[20] Mark 1:34; 1:39; 3:15; 6:13; 7:26; 9:18; 9:28; 9:38; 16:9; 16:17.

[21] Luke 9:40; 9:49; 11:14; 11:15; 11:18; 11:19; 11:20; 13:32.

[22] John 12:31.

[23] Bible Works, computer software, Friberg Lexicon, version 4.0

[24] Mark 1:25; 5:8; 9:25; Luke 4:35; 8:29; Acts 16:18.

[25] Mark 1:25; 5:8; 9:25; Luke 4:35.

The word *epitimaō*, while being associated with exorcism is rarely used in the context of the demonic. The word *epitimaō* can mean to (a) rebuke or (b) command. It occurs twenty-nine times in the New Testament (in its various forms), being used once in the context of exorcism.[26] Jesus rebukes a demon to be silent and then commands the demon to come out. Likewise, the word *hypagō* is used seventy-nine times in the New Testament but only once in the context of exorcism.[27] The word *hypagō* can mean to (a) move along, (b) depart, (c) leave, (d) die, or (e) undergo.[28] Matthew records Jesus' use of the word *hypagō* in the Gergesa exorcism (found here in the imperative). In the context of exorcism, the word *paragnellō* is generally translated as "order" or "command." The word *paragnellō* occurs thirty-two times in the New Testament, twice in the context of exorcism.[29] In each of these cases, these Greek words may be used in connection with an exorcism, which is casting out or removing a spiritual entity from someone who is possessed. The Greek word used to describe possession is *daimonizomai*. *Daimonizomai* can be properly translated as (a) demon possessed, (b) oppressed, or (c) to be tormented or vexed by a demon.[30] The word occurs twelve times in the Gospels and Acts.[31]

The Gospels establish exorcism. Jesus conducts exorcisms while at the same time He extends this command to His apostles. Moreover, it is clear from the texts that actual exorcisms occurred. Demons are cast out of people. The exorcisms of Jesus and His apostles did not escape the notice of the religious leaders of the time. They respond to Jesus' exorcisms by connecting them to the work of Satan. Jesus denies this and demonstrates the false logic of the Pharisees, Scribes, and Sadducees who falsely accuse Him. It is not by the power of Satan that Jesus operates but by the power of God. Jesus responds,

---

[26] Mark 9:25.

[27] Matthew 8:32.

[28] Bible Works, computer software, Friberg Lexicon, version 4.0.

[29] Luke 8:29; Acts 16:18.

[30] Bible Works, computer software, Friberg Lexicon, version 4.0.

[31] Matthew 4:24; 8:16; 8:28; 8:33; 9:32; 12:22; Mark 1:32; 5:15; 5:16; 5:18; Luke 8:36; John 10:21.

"But if it is by the Spirit of God that I cast out demons, then the kingdom of God has come upon you."[32]

THE KINGDOM OF GOD AND THE FALL OF SATAN

As the Gospel is proclaimed throughout the world, Jesus continues to drive back Satan and his forces.

—Jeffrey Gibbs

The Kingdom of God is one of the main themes of the Gospels. Where the Kingdom of God exists, Satan has no power and must flee. The demons, which once brought fear to the people, now shout out in the dread of their own existence, "What have you to do with us, O Son of God? Have you come here to torment us before the time?"[33] The demons of the New Testament Scriptures recognized Jesus' authority;[34] moreover, both Jesus and His apostles accept the validity of both the demonic and demoniacal possession. Yet, many modern theologians find it difficult to accept the biblical account, not to mention any possibility of modern-day occurrences of demonic possession.[35] The New Testament commentator R. C. H. Lenski recognizes the problems of modern theology as he writes:

> Why did not a single man of the ancient world understand them so? Are we becoming wiser? Then let us congratulate ourselves on our good fortune; but we cannot on that account compel these venerable writers to say what in their own time they neither could nor would say.[36]

Lenski's question is a compelling one not only for theologians, but also for anyone who turns to the Bible and questions these things. "Are we becoming wiser?" that is, wiser than the divinely inspired authors, namely, Matthew, Mark, Luke, and John. Many think they

---

[32] Matthew 12:28.

[33] Matthew 8:29.

[34] The authority of Jesus does not come from ancient artifacts or libraries of incantations. Graham H. Twelftree, *Jesus the Exorcist: a Contribution to the Study of the Historical Jesus* (Peabody, MA: Hendrickson, 1993), 82.

[35] Sorensen, *Possession and Exorcism*, 117.

[36] Lenski, *The Interpretation of St. Matthew's Gospel*, 175.

are wiser and more sophisticated about such things. Today, Seminaries education rarely discusses the topic of demon possession or exorcism. It is my hope that this section of the book restarts the conversation, not only within academia, but also in sermons, bible studies, and general pastoral care.

If demons and demoniacal possession were realities experienced by the apostolic writers, how can anyone suggest that such things do not continue to occur? Jeffrey Gibbs, professor of exegetical theology at Concordia Seminary is one of the few modern theologians that have begun to readdress the question of demon possession. In Volume One of his commentary on Matthew, Gibbs writes:

> The Scriptures affirm that in Christ's earthly ministry and continuing throughout the NT era, Satan is bound to an extent (Mt 12:22–29; Rev 20:2), so that he cannot prevent the Gospel from being proclaimed (Mt 24:14; 2 Tim 2:24–26). Toward the end of this age, Satan will be let loose for a short time (Rev 20:3). Moreover, the Scriptures picture Satan as being thrown out of heaven and defeated by the earthly ministry of Jesus, culminating in his death and resurrection (Lk 10:18; Jn 12:31; Col 2:15; Rev 12:5–10). As the Gospel is proclaimed throughout the world, Jesus continues to drive back Satan and his forces. Therefore, it should not surprise us if demonic possession is much rarer in our world and in our experience than it seems to have been in Palestine during Jesus' ministry. Jesus' numerous encounters with the demoniacs in the Synoptic Gospels testify that the time of his earthly ministry was unique in all the history of the creation . . . Nevertheless, Scripture does not declare that such things as oppression and even possession by demons are impossible or unknown during this present time, perhaps especially among peoples and in lands where the Gospel has not yet been proclaimed widely or at all.[37]

Gibbs reminds his readers that there will also come a time when Satan is "loosed" to work his evil upon men. Has this occurred in our time or does this continue to be a coming event? If the Malagasy Lutherans were to answer this question, they may answer in the

---

[37] Gibbs, *Matthew 1:1–11:1*, 453.

affirmative. Daily the exorcists of the Malagasy Lutheran Church continue to drive out demons that have possessed the people. Why do so many within the Western Church continue to deny something that is so clearly confessed throughout Holy Scripture? The biblical witness is clear and full. The remainder of this chapter will take the reader through the overwhelming evidence of diabolical possession in the New Testament and the significance of exorcism in the ministry of Jesus and the apostles.

EXORCISM IN THE GOSPEL OF MATTHEW AND ITS PARALLELS

God has broken into history, through exorcism and in healing, so as to rule graciously through Jesus.

—Jeffrey Gibbs

Exorcisms are common in Matthew's Gospel. In this section, we will travel through all of the occurrences of exorcism found in Matthew's Gospel. The parallel text (similar accounts from the other Gospels) will also be included in each section to provide context with the other apostolic witness.

MATTHEW 7:15–23

The first occurrence of the Greek verb referring to exorcism (*ekballō*) is found in Matthew 7:22.[38] Jesus warns His disciples that the ability of casting out demons in His name does not guarantee personal heavenly acceptance. The context begins in Matthew 7:15 as Jesus says:

Beware of false prophets, who come to you in sheep's clothing but inwardly are ravenous wolves. You will recognize them by their fruits. Are grapes gathered from thorn bushes, or figs from thistles? So, every healthy tree bears good fruit, but the diseased tree bears bad fruit. A healthy tree cannot bear bad fruit, nor can a diseased tree bear

---

[38] Earlier in 4:24, Matthew informs his readers that one aspect of Jesus' ministry was exorcism. However, in this case the word *exorcism* is not used. Instead, Matthew connects the demonized with the healing aspect of Jesus' ministry.

good fruit. Every tree that does not bear good fruit is cut down and thrown into the fire. Thus you will recognize them by their fruits. "Not everyone who says to Me, 'Lord, Lord,' will enter the kingdom of heaven, but the one who does the will of My Father who is in heaven.[39]

Following these remarks Jesus then adds:

On that day, many will say to Mme, "Lord, Lord, did we not prophesy in Your name, and cast out demons in Your name, and do many mighty works in Your name?" Then will I declare to them, "I never knew you; depart from Me, you workers of lawlessness."[40]

It is interesting that Matthew begins his treatment of exorcism with a warning . . . [41] Matthew records Jesus as condemning those who are performing exorcisms in his name. The problem is not the formula they are using, but the fact that they lack faith and act in their own interest. Previous acts or works do not guarantee future faithfulness.[42] These exorcists were not concerned with the work of Jesus, but only their own works.[43] We must take such warnings seriously, whenever we consider exorcism or the possibility of its use in the church today. Yet, the form of exorcism used in this passage is simple and direct, namely, the name of Jesus. These exorcists were driving out demons by invoking the name of Jesus. Using the name of Jesus will continue to be a formula used in all of the exorcisms found in the scriptures.

---

[39] Matthew 7:15–21.

[40] Matthew 7:22–23.

[41] Graham H. Twelftree, *In the Name of Jesus: Exorcism among Early Christians* (Grand Rapids: Baker Academic, 2007), 161.

[42] "While the Lord may have used someone on many occasions to cast out demons from other individuals this does not ensure escape from the devil for that individual. Pride is a weapon that Satan continually uses to trap those who have previously done great works for the Church." R. C. H. Lenski, *The Interpretation of St. Luke's Gospel*, 584.

[43] Twelftree, *In the Name of Jesus*, 163.

MATTHEW 8:16–17 (MARK 1:32–34)

The fact that Jesus was well-known as an exorcist is established in this text: "That evening they brought to him many who were oppressed by demons, and he cast out the spirits with a word and healed all who were sick."[44] Jesus is fulfilling the work that Matthew has already described in 4:24 however, now Matthew connects Jesus' work to the Old Testament. He tells his readers, "This was to fulfill what was spoken by the prophet Isaiah: 'He took our illnesses and bore our diseases.' "[45] Matthew understands exorcism as a positive action, which brings healing to individuals who were literally "oppressed by demons." By connecting Jesus' exorcistic work to the Old Testament's portrait of the Messiah, Matthew demonstrates that the origins of exorcism are already in the Old Testament. Matthew reports Jesus' exorcisms as the fulfillment of Isaiah's prophecy.[46] Gibbs agrees. He writes:

> God has broken into history, through exorcism and in healing, so as to rule graciously through Jesus. Satan will be defeated, and Jesus is driving back the effects of sin as the one who has come to save his people from their sins (Mt 1:21) . . . In Matthew 8:16–17 the evangelist interprets Jesus' deeds of power. The purpose of Jesus' healings and exorcism was to fulfill what was spoken by Isaiah the prophet: "he himself took our sickness, and carried our diseases."[47]

Exorcism is a necessary reality for Matthew. This text is preparation for his readers. Matthew will soon provide five occurrences of exorcism.[48] Mark 1:32–34 provides a parallel text to Matthew 8:16–17:

> That evening at sundown, they brought to Him all who were sick or oppressed by demons. And the whole city was gathered together at the door. And He healed many who were sick with various diseases, and cast out many demons. And

---

[44] Matthew 8:16.

[45] Matthew 8:17; Isaiah 53:12.

[46] Isaiah 53:4.

[47] Gibbs, *Matthew 1:1–11:1*, 424.

[48] Matthew 8:28–34; 9:33–35; 12:22; 15:21–25; 17:14–20.

He would not permit the demons to speak because they knew Him.[49]

Mark demonstrates the reality of demonic possession in this text; however, in Mark's version when the demons are confronted with the power and authority of Jesus, they are bound by His powerful word.

MATTHEW 8:28–34 (MARK 5:1–20, LUKE 8:26–39)

The first exorcism Matthew chooses to present to his readers is one of the most extraordinary exorcisms performed by Jesus. All three of the Synoptic Gospels report this event.[50] When Matthew tells this story, unlike the events found in Mark and Luke, he does not dwell on the conversation between Jesus and the demon-possessed men.[51] The demons see Jesus approaching and identify Him quickly as the Son of God. Next, the demons beg Him to send them away into the herd of swine.[52] Jesus was in control. The demons could do nothing but beg.[53] The demons are so fearful of exorcism that they themselves say, "If you cast us out, send us away into the herd of pigs."[54] They know that they cannot sustain their position before Jesus; indeed, they are anticipating exorcisms. In Matthew's account, Jesus simply says "go" or "depart," and they do. They come out of the men and enter into the swine.[55] Jesus commands these demons to depart and they flee.[56]

The parallel texts connected to Matthew 8:28–34 are Mark 5:1–20 and Luke 8:26–39 These texts share many similarities with Matthew's account, the first being the location. While Matthew records the area of the Gadarenes as the location, most scholars have concluded that the Synoptic Gospels refer to the same geographic

---

[49] Mark 1:32–34.

[50] Matthew 8:28–34; Mark 5:1–20; Luke 8:26–39.

[51] Dale Allison and W. D. Davies, *A Critical and Exegetical Commentary On The Gospel According to Saint Matthew*, vol. 2. (T&T Clark: Edinburgh, 1998), 82.

[52] Matthew 8:31.

[53] Gibbs, *Matthew 1:1–11:1*, 451.

[54] Matthew 8:31.

[55] Matthew 8:32.

[56] Gibbs, *Matthew 1:1–11:1*, 451.

area (Gergesa) which is Kursi in modern geography.[57] The next similarity the three parallels share is in each case the demons come to meet Jesus. Jesus does not need to go looking for them. Moreover, the demons knew exactly who Jesus was, the Son of God.[58] Finally, each of the parallels end with the demons being cast into the swine and running to their death into the water at the bottom of the hill.

If one were to read the popular material found in bookstores dealing with exorcism, one would find modern exorcist describing the necessity of questioning the demon as to their name and the reasons they possessed their host, but such questioning is foreign to the Gospels. In Matthew's Gospel, Jesus speaks very little to the demons.[59] He does not question the demons; He simply tells them to depart. Jesus commands the evil spirits to depart, and they leave their hosts. However, it is true that in both the Gospels of Mark and Luke Jesus is found questioning the demons. He asks them for their names, and they respond, "Legion," which the authors then tell us means that many demons had entered the man. This demonstrates that it is possible for many demons to enter into and dwell within an individual. However, to suggest that others involved in exorcisms are required to perform such questioning of the demons is overreaching the bounds of the text.

MATTHEW 9:32–33 (MATTHEW 12:22–24, MARK 3:7–30, LUKE 11:24–26)

The next exorcism found in Matthew's Gospel is located in the ninth chapter. Little can be determined concerning this particular exorcism. Only two verses speak the exorcism. Matthew writes:

---

[57] In 2000, I traveled to this area and made the following conclusions. Gadara was the capital city of the toparch (the ruler of a small state or realm), about six miles southeast of the Sea of Galilee, a distance that would have taken more than two hours to reach by foot from the shore of the Sea of Galilee. Therefore, the possibility of the city of Gadara as the place for this event must be put to rest. On the other hand, the small city of Gergesa is located just across the Sea from Capernaum. It therefore fits the first criteria of all of our Gospel accounts. It is on the shore of the Sea and a large cliff is adjacent to the site. This is the only such cliff found anywhere on the east side of the Sea. Gergesa has also been recognized by tradition as the site for the demoniac's healing.

[58] Matthew 8:29; Mark 5:7; Luke 8:28.

[59] Refer to the Matthew section for additional details.

As they were going away, behold, a demon-oppressed man who was mute was brought to Him. And when the demon had been cast out, the mute man spoke. And the crowds marveled, saying, "Never was anything like this seen in Israel."[60]

This passage demonstrates three points: the demon made the man mute, there was an exorcism, and the people were amazed as a result of the exorcism. This text also demonstrates that physical defects can be the result of demonic activity within an individual. Finally, this exorcism produced an evangelistic result, that is, the people were amazed, and as a result, many put their trust in the Lord. However, the Pharisees did not share this amazement. They understood Jesus' exorcistic activities as a work of evil. "But the Pharisees said, 'He casts out demons by the prince of demons.' "[61] The Pharisees will not give up on this line of reasoning. In chapter twelve of Matthew's Gospel, Jesus is once again accused of being in alliance with a demonic figure known as Beelzebub/Beelzebul:[62]

Then a demon-oppressed man who was blind and mute was brought to Him, and He healed him so that the man spoke and saw. And all the people were amazed and said, "Can this be the Son of David?" But when the Pharisees heard it, they said, "It is only by Beelzebub, the prince of demons that this man casts out demons."[63]

There was no doubt that Jesus had been performing numerous exorcisms. His activity had not escaped the notice of the religious leaders. It was becoming a problem for them, so much so, that they found it necessary to distract the people by calling Jesus' work evil and connecting Him to "Beelzebub, the prince of demons."[64] This led Jesus to present a rebuttal showing the inconsistency of the Pharisees' argument, and at the same time, teaching His hearers what actually occurs in exorcism:

---

[60] Matthew 9:32–33.

[61] Matthew 9:34.

[62] For background and additional study relating to the title Beelzebul, see Craig S. Keener, *IVP Bible Background Commentary New Testament* (Downers Grove: InterVarsity Press, 1993), 80.

[63] Matthew 12:22–24.

[64] Matthew 12:24.

Knowing their thoughts, He said to them, "Every kingdom divided against itself is laid waste, and no city or house divided against itself will stand. And if Satan casts out Satan, he is divided against himself. How then will his kingdom stand? And if I cast out demons by Beelzebub, by whom do your sons cast them out? Therefore, they will be your judges. But if it is by the Spirit of God that I cast out demons, then the kingdom of God has come upon you. Or how can someone enter a strong man's house and plunder his goods, unless he first binds the strong man? Then indeed, he may plunder his house."[65]

In these words, Jesus is declaring His divinity and power. Each exorcism Jesus performs becomes a sign that the kingdom of Satan is crumbling.[66] The Kingdom of God has come upon them.[67] There is no room for evil or Satan in the presence of the Son of God. Jesus is stronger than the strong man, known as Satan, and he, namely Satan, is being driven out wherever Jesus is found. However, Jesus also offers a warning to those freed from the demonic grasp. He says:

When the unclean spirit has gone out of a person, it passes through waterless places seeking rest but finds none. Then it says, "I will return to my house from which I came." And when it comes, it finds the house empty, swept, and put in order. Then it goes and brings with it seven other spirits more evil than itself, and they enter and dwell there, and the last state of that person is worse than the first.[68]

Only Matthew and Luke add this additional ending. Consequently, these texts are significant because they give the reader insight into the reality of possession and exorcism, thus showing that multiple demons can reside within an individual. Additionally, without the presence of the Holy Spirit the individual can experience a greater state of possession with each successive exorcism.

---

[65] Matthew 12:25–29; Luke 11:24–26.

[66] Twelftree finds Matthew linking the exorcisms of Jesus with the two-stage defeat of Satan. See Twelftree, *In the Name of Jesus*, 169.

[67] Matthew 12:28.

[68] Matthew 12:43–45; Luke 11:26.

The parallel to this text is Mark 3:7–30. The text contains three separate sections relating to one another. The first begins by reporting that the demons continued to show anxiety whenever Jesus confronted them.[69] The demons were crying out and revealing Jesus' identity by calling Him the "Son of God."[70] To the demons, there was no doubt who stood before them. Moreover, Jesus demonstrates this authority by "strictly ordering them not to make Him known."[71]

The next section of the text deals specifically with the apostles. Jesus is about to command them to become exorcists:

> And He went up on the mountain and called to Him those whom He desired, and they came to Him. And He appointed twelve (whom He also named apostles) so that they might be with Him and He might send them out to preach and have authority to cast out demons.[72]

Here, Mark clearly demonstrates that Jesus did not reserve exorcism for His own use but that the vocation of apostle included the healing gift of exorcism. Verses 16–19 simply list the apostles that were to receive this power.[73]

The final section of this text deals with the reception of Jesus' power of exorcism by two extremely different groups: His family and the scribes.[74] Jesus' family thought Him insane.[75] They wanted to take Him away. Their actions relate to those of the scribes; however, their motives are different. The family is seeking to protect Jesus while the scribes are seeking to discredit Him and finally murder Him. While the family finds sickness, the scribes find malice. Therefore, they

---

[69] Mark 3:7–12.

[70] Mark 3:11.

[71] Mark 3:12.

[72] Mark 3:13–15; Matthew 10:2–4.

[73] Mark 3:16–19.

[74] Mark 3:20–30.

[75] "The Greek word *exestē* (Indicative, aorist, active, 3rd person, singular) when used intransitively (all middle forms, second aorist active, and perfect active) and figuratively means to 'lose one's mind, be insane, be out of one's senses.' At other times the word can simply mean to be astonished." Bible Works, computer software, Friberg Lexicon, version 4.0 (Norfolk: Bible Works, 2007).

accuse Jesus of being possessed by Beelzebub and driving out demons "by the prince of demons."[76]

MATTHEW 10:1, 7–11, 14 (MARK 6:6B–13, LUKE 9:12)

While Matthew tends to present the failures of the apostles during their exorcistic endeavors, there is no doubt that Jesus intended His disciples to carry on His work of exorcism. By the time of the completion of the Synoptic Gospels, the church had been growing for more than twenty years.[77] The ascension had taken place, and the Holy Spirit had been sent out to the world to bring to remembrance all that Jesus had done and taught.[78] In each case, the command is clear. Jesus calls the apostles and gives them authority to cast out demons. Gibbs writes:

> Matthew makes it crystal clear that in the most fundamental sense, the mission work of the Twelve will only be an extension of Jesus' own ministry. They will minister in Israel with authority, but it will be the authority that Jesus has given them. Their authority will extend over unclean spirits that plague the people and over sickness and every disease; Jesus has demonstrated his own authority over those very foes in chapters 8 and 9, and the apostles' work will be manifestations of his own work.[79]

Exorcism is Jesus' work, and the apostles are included as His means of defeating Satan. As the apostles went out into the lands, they carried with them the words of Jesus, words that brought light into the valley of darkness.[80] Luke adds to the phrase, "power and authority," while Matthew and Mark speak of Jesus giving only "authority" over the demons. For Luke, the apostles not only have the authority to carry out their work, but also the power needed. Exegetical theologian William Arndt uses an example from a typical

---

[76] Mark 3:22.

[77] All of the dating for the New Testament will follow John A. T. Robinson's important work which provides conservative dates for all of the New Testament texts. See John Arthur Thomas Robinson, *Redating the New Testament* (New York: Wipf & Stock, 2000), 352.

[78] John 16:13.

[79] Gibbs, *Matthew 1:1–11:1*, 500.

[80] Isaiah 9:2.

parenting situation to demonstrate the difference between having authority with and without power. He writes:

> "Power" is the ability to do a certain thing; "authority" is the right to perform the act. Parents have authority to make their children obey them, but in all too many instances, they lack the power.[81]

Graham Twelftree, who writes a powerful book on the exorcisms of Jesus, understands Luke's Gospel to be a Gospel of power.[82] The power of the apostles resides in their preaching. They are speaking the word of Jesus, and with this word, there is the power to act. The parallel texts are included for reference, beginning with Matthew followed by Mark and Luke:

> And He called to Him His twelve disciples and gave them authority over unclean spirits, to cast them out, and to heal every disease and every affliction.[83]

> And He called the twelve and began to send them out two by two, and gave them authority over the unclean spirits.[84]

> And He called the twelve together and gave them power and authority over all demons and to cure diseases, and He sent them out to proclaim the kingdom of God and to heal.[85]

Luke also adds the word *power* and explains the purpose of this power and authority that Jesus bestows upon the apostles: they were sent out to proclaim the kingdom of God.[86] The kingdom of Satan was all but gone; Jesus had come, and His power and authority belong to God. Mark reports the success of the apostles. He writes, "And they cast out many demons and anointed with oil many who were sick and healed them."[87] Not only does Jesus purposely send out the

---

[81] William F. Arndt, *Luke* (St. Louis: Concordia, 1984), 250.

[82] Twelftree, *In the Name of Jesus*, 136.

[83] Matthew 10:1.

[84] Mark 6:7.

[85] Luke 9:1–2.

[86] Luke 9:2.

[87] Mark 6:13.

apostles as exorcists, but they also successfully perform the task given them.

MATTHEW 15:21–28 (MARK 7:24–30)

Both of these parallels handle this text in similar fashions. The demonic have a stronghold upon the Gentile nations; the daughter of the Syrophoenician is an excellent example of this activity:

> And from there he arose and went away to the region of Tyre and Sidon. And he entered a house and did not want anyone to know, yet he could not be hidden. But immediately a woman whose little daughter was possessed by an unclean spirit heard of him and came and fell down at his feet. Now the woman was a Gentile, a Syrophoenician by birth. And she begged him to cast the demon out of her daughter. And he said to her, "Let the children be fed first, for it is not right to take the children's bread and throw it to the dogs." But she answered him, "Yes, Lord; yet even the dogs under the table eat the children's crumbs." And he said to her, "For this statement you may go your way; the demon has left your daughter." And she went home and found the child lying in bed and the demon gone.[88]

This account is significant in at least three ways. First, Jesus heals the daughter of a Gentile. This is the first account that demonstrates Jesus' healing of a demoniac originating in a Gentile community.[89] This text also demonstrates that children may also become afflicted by demoniacal possession.[90] Finally, Jesus is not limited to locality. He does this healing from a distance. Matthew records Jesus' words: "O woman, great is your faith! Be it done for you as you desire." Her daughter was healed instantly.[91] Mark adds some additional details:

---

[88] Mark 7:24–30.

[89] Some might suppose that the Gergesa demoniac was a Gentile and therefore disagree that this is Jesus first exorcism of a Gentile. See Todd Klutz, *The Exorcism Stories in Luke-Acts A Sociostylistic Reading (Society for New Testament Studies Monograph Series)* (New York: Cambridge UP, 2004), 88.

[90] R. C. H. Lenski, *The Interpretation of St. Mark's Gospel* (Columbus: Wartburg Press, 1946), 302.

[91] Matthew 15:28.

And He said to her, "For this statement you may go your way; the demon has left your daughter." And she went home and found the child lying in bed and the demon gone.[92]

These texts agree, most of the healing, and all of the other exorcisms occur in Jesus' presence, this exorcism takes place over a long distance. Jesus' power over demons is ultimate and unlimited. His Word is the powerful and creative Word that, when spoken, creates a reality, the reality of healing, which is the defeat of Satan and his demons.

MATTHEW 17:14–20 (MARK 9:14–29, LUKE 9:37–45)

And when they came to the crowd, a man came up to Him and, kneeling before Him, said, "Lord, have mercy on my son, for he is an epileptic and he suffers terribly. For often he falls into the fire and often into the water. And I brought him to Your disciples, and they could not heal him." And Jesus answered, "O faithless and twisted generation, how long am I to be with you? How long am I to bear with you? Bring him here to Me." And Jesus rebuked him, and the demon came out of him, and the boy was healed instantly. Then the disciples came to Jesus privately and said, "Why could we not cast it out?" He said to them, "Because of your little faith. For truly, I say to you, if you have faith like a grain of mustard seed, you will say to this mountain, 'Move from here to there,' and it will move, and nothing will be impossible for you." (Matthew 17:14–20)

The finial exorcism performed by Jesus in Matthew's Gospel occurs in chapter seventeen.[93] In this text, the disciples attempt to cast out a demon, but they fail.[94] They ask, "Why could we not cast it out?"[95] Jesus answers, "Because of your unbelief."[96] The disciples were beginning to form a mechanistic understanding (*ex opera operato*) of the Word. Was the work of exorcism becoming magic to

---

[92] Mark 7:29–30.

[93] Matthew 17:19.

[94] Matthew 17:14–19.

[95] Matthew 17:19, (verb, infinitive, aorist, active).

[96] Matthew 17:20.

them?[97] Had they forgotten that they had only been speaking in the stead of Jesus and by His authority and power? It appears so. This should be a caution to anyone called to speak Jesus' exorcist words. The power is Jesus' and He is the only exorcist.

Two more parallel texts require consideration: Mark 9:14–29 and Luke 9:37–45. It is true that Jesus had sent the apostles out with the mandate to cast out demons, but He had also warned them about their attitudes when doing His work.[98] Both of these texts share similarities with Matthew's Gospel. However, Mark and Luke do not use the word *epileptic* when describing the boy's condition as Matthew clearly does.[99]

Modern medicine has classified epilepsy as a physiological disease,[100] yet such terminology is unknown to the scriptures. Lenski writes:

> At the sight of Jesus the demon becomes enraged and vents his horrible power upon his victim. . . . These are the symptoms of an epileptic fit: falling to the ground, continuing to wallow, twisting and turning on the ground, and foaming at the mouth . . . Note this is not a case of ordinary epilepsy. Such persons are not thrown into a fit by the mere sight of another person. The demon is explicitly named as causing a violent fit. This is perfectly in line with all else that the Gospel writers report about possession; the demons cause dumbness and deafness besides epilepsy.[101]

The demon causes a fit for the purpose of bringing harm to the young boy.[102] William Lane, a biblical commentator, finds such destruction to be the purpose of demoniacal possession.[103] However, Jesus will

---

[97] William F. Arndt, *Luke* (St. Louis: Concordia, 1984), 285.

[98] Luke 10:17–20.

[99] Matthew 17:14–20.

[100] For a discussion of the symptoms of epilepsy contrasted with demonic possession See Hans Naegeil Osjord, *Possession & Exorcism* (Oregon: New Frontiers Center, 1988), 34.

[101] Lenski, *The Interpretation of St. Mark's Gospel*, 379.

[102] Lenski, *The Interpretation of St. Mark's Gospel*, 384.

[103] William L. Lane, *The Gospel According to Mark* (Grand Rapids: Eerdmans, 1974), 331.

not allow this to happen. After pausing to denounce the faith of the apostles, Jesus moves forward with the exorcism. Once again, with a simple word Jesus drives the demon away. Why had the apostles failed? Why were they unable to exorcise the demon? Mark, just as Matthew, answers this question with the following words:

> And when He had entered the house, His disciples asked Him privately, "Why could we not cast it out?" And He said to them, "This kind cannot be driven out by anything but prayer."[104]

This exorcism required prayer, but for prayer to be effective, faith is also necessary.[105] Once again, exorcism is the result of Jesus' work—not the apostles'. Jesus performed all of the exorcisms, even those done through the command of the apostles. Did the apostles fail because they were trying to drive out the demon with their own power, rather than that of Jesus? One possibility is that they had begun to lose their way and their focus. Whatever the case, upon their failure, Jesus said, "O faithless generation, how long am I to be with you?"[106] Without faith, there is no power to exorcise.[107] The power to drive out demons resides in Jesus, that is, in His name. Simply speaking the name is not enough. The command to "depart" must be spoken in the faith that Jesus will be the active force in the exorcism. While Jesus has commanded the apostles to be exorcists, they are ones who are under authority. However, I suggest that they had lost faith in the authority that they had been given.[108] It is Jesus' authority which effects healing, not just the recitation of His name.

---

[104] Mark 9:28–29.

[105] Matthew 17:20.

[106] Matthew 17:17; Mark 9:19; Luke 9:41.

[107] Lenski, *The Interpretation of St. Mark's Gospel*, 386.

[108] Lenski, *The Interpretation of St. Mark's Gospel*, 385.

EXORCISM IN THE GOSPEL OF MARK
AND LUKAN PARALLELS

He commands even the unclean spirits, and they obey Him. And at once His fame spread everywhere throughout all the surrounding region of Galilee.

—Mark 1:27–28

MARK 1:21–28 (LUKE 4:31–41)

The first miracle recorded in both Mark and Luke is that of an exorcism.[109] The beginning of Mark's Gospel demonstrates the prominence of Jesus' exorcisms. Jesus is teaching in a synagogue when a demon-possessed man identifies Him as the "Holy one of God." The demons are correct; Jesus is the "Holy one of God" just as they are correct in their description of Jesus' motive. Jesus has come to "destroy them." Jesus' presence among the demons had begun their downfall.[110] Jesus commands the demons to come out of the man:

> And they went into Capernaum, and immediately on the Sabbath He entered the synagogue and was teaching. And they were astonished at His teaching, for He taught them as one who had authority, and not as the scribes. And immediately there was in their synagogue a man with an unclean spirit. And he cried out, "What have you to do with us, Jesus of Nazareth? Have you come to destroy us? I know who You are—the Holy One of God." But Jesus rebuked him, saying, "Be silent, and come out of him!" And the unclean spirit, convulsing him and crying out with a loud voice, came out of him. And they were all amazed so that they questioned among themselves, saying, "What is this? A new teaching with authority! He commands even the unclean spirits, and they obey Him." And at once His fame spread

---

[109] See Larry W. Hurtado, *Lord Jesus Christ: Devotion to Jesus in Earliest Christianity* (Boston: Eerdmans, 2003), 178.

[110] Lane, *The Gospel According to Mark*, 75.

everywhere throughout all the surrounding region of Galilee.[111]

This is only the beginning for Mark. Mark selects this as Jesus' first miracle. He does this so Jesus may be exposed as the Messiah early on, without the necessity of a birth narrative as found in Matthew and Luke.[112] It is also significant, that while Matthew records five exorcisms, Mark records eight.[113] Mark's Gospel presents Jesus as the one with authority over the evil forces in the world. Jesus simply speaks, and the demons are helpless. Lenski rightfully identifies the power of preaching with exorcism. The preached word always brings the defeat of Satan and his forces of evil.[114]

MARK 9:38–39 (LUKE 9:49–50)

The authority of Jesus' name is not the point of this text, yet there is much here to learn concerning the form of exorcism used by the apostles. The context concerns someone we presume to be a believer, who is casting out demons by using the name of Jesus. Both Mark and Luke follow one another very closely.[115] Mark's text is provided for brevity. Mark records John's words:

> John said to Him, "Teacher, we saw someone casting out demons in Your name, and we tried to stop him, because he was not following us." But Jesus said, "Do not stop him, for no one who does a mighty work in My name will be able soon afterward to speak evil of Me. For the one who is not against us is for us."[116]

It appears that the problem John had with these other "Christian exorcists" was misplaced. He says that they tried to stop this man because "he was not following us . . ."[117] John was attempting to prevent the man from acting because he was envious. Jesus responds,

---

[111] Mark 1:21–28.

[112] Lenski, *The Interpretation of St. Mark's Gospel*, 80.

[113] Mark 1:21–28; 1:32–34; 3:7–30; 5:1–20; 6:7–13; 7:24–30; 9:14–29; 9:38–39.

[114] Lenski, *The Interpretation of St. Mark's Gospel*, 81.

[115] Mark 9:38–39; Luke 9:49–50.

[116] Mark 9:38–40.

[117] Mark 9:38; Luke 9:49.

"Do not stop him, for no one who does a mighty work in My name will be able soon afterward to speak evil of Me."[118] From these words, we conclude that this "unauthorized" exorcist may have been effective in his work. This text demonstrates the process employed by the early Christians as they sought to cast out demons. They did so with a simple command, with little pomp or show. They commanded the demons to depart in Jesus' name. Moreover, this process was proving to be effective. The demons were departing because the name of Jesus was used in faith. The commonality of exorcism in the Early Church may have partially been behind the early devotional use of Jesus' name.[119] Much of the devotion to Jesus' name would have come from the remembrance of the power it brought to the apostles. The name had power, not as an incantation, but as a connection to Jesus' very person.[120]

EXORCISM IN THE GOSPEL OF LUKE AND ACTS

The seventy-two returned with joy, saying, "Lord, even the demons are subject to us in Your name!"

—Luke 10:17

LUKE 8:1–3 (MARK 16:9)

In this section, the text is examined through Luke's perspective, although a parallel is found in Mark chapter sixteen.[121] This text is remarkably short and reveals very little about Mary Magdalene's previous demonic problems. The text simply states:

Soon afterward He went on through cities and villages, proclaiming and bringing the good news of the kingdom of God. And the twelve were with Him, and also some women who had been healed of evil spirits and infirmities: Mary, called Magdalene, from whom seven demons had gone out and Joanna, the wife of Chuza, Herod's household manager,

---

[118] Mark 9:39; Luke 9:50.

[119] Hurtado, *Lord Jesus Christ: Devotion to Jesus in Earliest Christianity*, 204–205.

[120] Revelation 3:12; 22:4.

[121] Mark 16:9.

and Susanna, and many others, who provided for them out of their means.[122]

Luke uses the plural: Jesus is traveling with women, "who had been healed of evil spirits and infirmities." Yet, Mary Magdalene is the only woman who is specifically described as being previously demon possessed. This event is significant because it portrays at least one, if not more, of the prominent followers of Jesus as previously afflicted by demoniacal possession.

There is a significant connection found in this text with the *Fifohazana* movement of the Malagasy Lutheran Church. Many of those serving in the Malagasy Lutheran Church identify themselves as previously being in bondage to Satan and his demons. They have become faithful followers of Jesus because Jesus has freed them from the bondage of servitude, which they had previously owed to Satan. Now they have become servants of Jesus, the only true Lord.

LUKE 10:1–17

This text is specific to Luke's Gospel. It describes the sending out of the seventy-two. While there has been some hinting through the Gospels that other disciples were also conducting exorcisms, Luke presents the seventy-two as being commissioned to become exorcists. There commissioning was similar to that which the apostles had received.[123] Luke demonstrates that these lay exorcists were effective. He writes:

> The seventy-two returned with joy, saying, "Lord, even the demons are subject to us in Your name!" And He said to them, "I saw Satan fall like lightning from heaven. Behold, I have given you authority to tread on serpents and scorpions, and over all the power of the enemy, and nothing shall hurt you. Nevertheless, do not rejoice in this, that the spirits are subject to you, but rejoice that your names are written in heaven."[124]

These disciples are almost too effective. They return to Jesus rejoicing about their success. About this, Jesus warns them,

---

[122] Luke 8:1–3.

[123] Matthew 10:1; Mark 6:7; Luke 9:1–2.

[124] Luke 10:17–20.

"Nevertheless, do not rejoice in this, that the spirits are subject to you, but rejoice that your names are written in heaven."[125] Exorcisms are for the present; they bring the Kingdom of God into the world by casting out the kingdom of Satan.[126] Jesus says, "I saw Satan fall like lightning from heaven."[127] Satan's first expulsion was from heaven, but now he is facing his second expulsion as Jesus begins the destruction of his earthly kingdom.[128] Yet, the followers of Jesus should not put their hope in the power they see demonstrated through their work, but instead in Christ, who will give them the eternal kingdom.

ACTS 16:16–18

Acts chapter sixteen (and later chapter nineteen) demonstrates that demon possession continues into the church age. In Acts chapter sixteen, Luke gives an example of a post-pentecostal exorcism. A young slave girl possessed by a demon is continually harassing Paul. She has the ability to tell the future. A demon gave her the abilities she was demonstrating before the people. Luke writes:

> As we were going to the place of prayer, we were met by a slave girl who had a spirit of divination and brought her owners much gain by fortune-telling. She followed Paul and us, crying out, "These men are servants of the Most High God, who proclaim to you the way of salvation." And this she kept doing for many days. Paul, having become greatly annoyed, turned and said to the spirit, "I command you in the name of Jesus Christ to come out of her." And it came out that very hour.[129]

First, this text demonstrates that demon possession continues into the Church age. Second, this text demonstrates that the form of exorcism Paul uses is consistent with that displayed in the Gospel

---

[125] Luke 10:20.

[126] Arndt understands, "every expulsion of a demon resulted in the fall of Satan." Arndt, *Luke*, 242.

[127] Luke 10:18.

[128] There are varying ways to understand this text. Some describe this fall of Satan in the exorcisms and healings of the seventy-two, Arndt, *Luke*, 285. "Others view it as an eschatological fall." Lenski, *The Interpretation of St. Luke's Gospel*, 580.

[129] Acts 16:16–18.

accounts. Paul casts out the demon in the name of Jesus Christ. The post-pentecostal Church continues in the same fashion as it did in the time of Jesus' earthly ministry. Jesus remains the "active one" in every exorcism. Paul does not need special rituals or artifacts; the name of Jesus spoken by one of His faithful followers is all that is required to send Satan and his demons on the run. Paul has both the authority and the power to act. It is an apostolic authority given to the apostles and passed on to the Church. Yet, the text demonstrates one additional item. Exorcism does not take place at the moment the words are spoken by Paul (*ex opere operato*). The text states, "And it came out that very hour."[130] This implies a time-lapse. It is possible that Luke includes this detail so that no magical implication is found.[131]

The exorcisms of the New Testament are not magic. The power to exorcise demons does not reside within individuals, and the words used are not some sort of secret phrases that can be learned or purchased. Jesus is the actor in all true exorcisms. He has come into the world to bind the "strong man." Exorcism in the name of Jesus is not something to toy with this becomes clear in the next section.

ACTS 19:13–19

In this text, Luke presents seven exorcists that he identifies as sons of a Jewish priest named Sceva. It is interesting that Luke uses a technical term for these men; he calls them exorcists, "those who drive out evil spirits, usually by invoking supernatural persons or powers or by the use of magic formulas."[132] The story is quite humorous:

> Then some of the itinerant Jewish exorcists undertook to invoke the name of the Lord Jesus over those who had evil spirits, saying, "I adjure you by the Jesus, whom Paul proclaims." Seven sons of a Jewish high priest named Sceva were doing this. But the evil spirit answered them, "Jesus I know, and Paul I recognize, but who are you?" And the man

---

[130] Acts 16:18.

[131] Acts 8:18–24. For additional information on the magical practices of Simon Magus, see Arland J. Hultgren and Steven A. Haggmark, eds., *The Earliest Christian Heretics Readings from their Opponents* (Minneapolis: Fortress Press, 1996), 15.

[132] Bible Works, computer software, Friberg Lexicon, version 4.0.

in whom was the evil spirit leaped on them, mastered all of them and overpowered them so that they fled out of that house naked and wounded. And this became known to all the residents of Ephesus, both Jews and Greeks. And fear fell upon them all, and the name of the Lord Jesus was extolled. Also, many of those who were now believers came, confessing and divulging their practices. And a number of those who had practiced magic arts brought their books together and burned them in the sight of all.[133]

The name of Jesus is not a magical incantation that can be used by individuals. Those who heard about His story clearly realized this truth. It appears that syncretism or the mixing of religions was also a problem in the Early Church. Many of those who had believed in Jesus continued to hold to their previous magical practices. However, the failed exorcism of the seven sons of Sceva demonstrated to the people that such practices had no value. This event caused a great increase in the Early Church, as Luke writes, "So the word of the Lord continued to increase and prevail mightily."[134] The Word of the Lord is not magic. The Word of the Lord brings the Lord Himself. While Jesus has commanded His followers to use His name, that name can never be separated from the one who carries it, namely, Jesus Christ, the Lord, the Son of God.

EXORCISM IN THE GOSPEL OF JOHN

Now is the judgment of this world; now will the ruler of this world be cast out.

—John 12:31

JOHN 12:31–37

While it may appear that John has little to say about exorcism, such an assumption would be ill-suited. To be sure, John has only one exorcism recorded in his Gospel, but it is the exorcism *par-excellence*. The exorcism found in John's Gospel is a culmination of

---

[133] Acts 19:13–19.

[134] Acts 19:20.

126

all the other exorcisms found within the New Testament scriptures. It is the ultimate picture of the spiritual battle waged upon the earth:

> [Jesus said] "Now is the judgment of this world; now will the ruler of this world be cast out. And I, when I am lifted up from the earth, will draw all people to Myself." He said this to show by what kind of death He was going to die. So the crowd answered Him, "We have heard from the Law that the Christ remains forever. How can you say that the Son of Man must be lifted up? Who is this Son of Man?" So Jesus said to them, "The light is among you for a little while longer. Walk while you have the light, lest darkness overtake you. The one who walks in the darkness does not know where he is going. While you have the light, believe in the light, that you may become sons of light." When Jesus had said these things, He departed and hid Himself from them. Though He had done so many signs before them, they still did not believe in Him . . . [135]

Here is the ultimate exorcism. Jesus is pointing to His own death upon the cross as an act of exorcism.[136] At the cross, Jesus will cast out (exorcize) Satan. The accuser of men will lose his power because all sin is exonerated in Jesus' death. Jesus describes the casting out of Satan as a future event. Lenski demonstrates the significance of this text:

> The future tense, "shall be thrown out," is punctiliar (relating to a point of time.) This is not a gradual pressing back of his control that runs its course through the centuries until the day of judgment, but a sudden dethronement in the hour that is now at hand. The devil receives his doom in the death and the resurrection of Jesus.[137]

---

[135] John 12:31–37.

[136] Marianne Meye Thompson, *The Incarnate Word: Perspectives on Jesus in the Fourth Gospel* (New York: Hendrickson, 1993), 94.

[137] Lenski, *The Interpretation of John's Gospel*, 874.

Satan is the "prince of this world," but at the cross, the prince is removed from his throne.[138] This expulsion should not be understood as a casting out from heaven, but rather as a casting out as ruler of this world.[139] Satan and his demons are not removed from the earth, but dislodged from their previous reign, a reign they have unlawfully seized. Lenski continues:

> Not that the world is now wholly rid of the devil and goes on with him being completely removed. The judgment on his kingdom ("this world") is the judgment on his rule over this kingdom, the decree that throws him out. What remains for him is the hopeless attempt of an already dethroned ruler to maintain himself in a kingdom, the very existence of which is blasted forever.[140]

Jesus warns the people that the darkness of Satan's operations will not disappear.[141] They are getting a reprieve, but also a warning. "The light is among you for a little while longer. Walk while you have the light, lest darkness overtake you."[142] While Satan is deeply wounded and eschatologically defeated, he continues to cause problems for the human race. Demon possession will continue, and Satan will attempt to hold control of his kingdom, but the deed is done.

---

[138] See Frank E. Gaebelein, *The Expositor's Bible Commentary: John and Acts*, vol. 9 (Grand Rapids: Zondervan, 1984), 130; and Leon Morris, *The Gospel According to John* (Grand Rapids: Eerdmans, 1995), 531.

[139] Ben Witherington, *John's Wisdom: A Commentary on the Fourth Gospel* (Louisville, KY: Westminster John Knox Press, 1995), 224.

[140] Lenski, *The Interpretation of John's Gospel*, 874.

[141] Gaebelein, *The Expositor's Bible Commentary*, 131; Morris, *The Gospel According to John*, 531; Witherington, *John's Wisdom A Commentary on the Fourth Gospel*, 225.

[142] John 12:35.

CHAPTER NINE

WE TREMBLE NOT

Though devils all the world should fill, all eager to devour us, we tremble not, we fear no ill, they shall never overpower us. . . one little word can fell him.

—Martin Luther

The Scriptures are clear: the devil is real and continues to bring destruction to the world and the people of God. The Church throughout history has accepted this premise. Martin Luther and the reformers continually identified the devil and his demons as the main force behind the false doctrines introduced into the Church. Luther and the Reformers still understood the devil to be the "prince of this world" even after his defeat by the crucifixion and resurrection of Jesus. This chapter focuses on the life of the Church and demonstrates the prevalence given to demonic activity throughout the time of the Reformation thru the time in which we now live. If you have thought otherwise, this chapter should remove any doubts you may have had up to this point.

We begin the examination of the continued use of demonic vocabulary and exorcism in the Church of the Reformation with the Confessions of the Lutheran Church as found in the Book of Concord. The words *devil*, *devils*, and *devilish* occur 228 times throughout the Lutheran Confessions.[1] A complete review of these texts is outside

---

[1] Theodore G. Tappert, *The Book of Concord: The Confessions of the Evangelical Lutheran Church* (New York: Augsburg Fortress, 1959). This includes both the Latin and German versions of the Augsburg Confession as translated by Tappert.

the scope of this book; therefore, only a limited number of references are examined.

LUTHER'S SMALCALD ARTICLES

Evil spirits have introduced the knavery of appearing as spirits of the departed and, with unspeakable lies and cunning, of demanding Masses, vigils, pilgrimages, and other alms.

—Martin Luther

Luther's understanding of the devil is particularly prevalent in the Smalcald Articles. Luther mentions the devil nineteen times in his Smalcald Articles. Part 2, Article 2 on the Mass proves to be a significant section that relates to Luther's understanding of the devil. Luther understands the Roman Mass as one of the most horrific works of Satan. The Mass, one of the greatest gifts of the Lord to His Church is turned into an idol used to lure men away from Christ and salvation. Luther writes, "The Mass in the papacy must be regarded as the greatest and most horrible abomination because it runs into direct and violent conflict with this fundamental article."[2] The Mass becomes a work of the devil. Moreover, the devil uses the Mass to control people. Luther writes about one of the consequences of the Mass:

> Evil spirits have introduced the knavery of appearing as spirits of the departed and, with unspeakable lies and cunning, of demanding Masses, vigils, pilgrimages, and other alms.[3]

Such a use of the Sacrament cannot be encouraged and leads the faithful away to the myths and lies of the devil. There is a connection here with the Malagasy traditional rite called *famadihana*. Many Malagasies describe the spirits of the departed appearing to them and asking for the *famadihana* service. There are many similarities between the spirits which Luther describes, who are demanding Masses, vigils, pilgrimages and other alms, and the *famadihana*,

---

[2] SA Part 2, Article 2, 1.

[3] SA Part 2, Article 2, 16.

which occur in the ancestor cults of Madagascar. During the time of Luther, people reported their deceased relatives were appearing to them and asking for these things to relieve or reduce their experience in purgatory. Many people of the time believed that such actions (Masses, vigils, pilgrimages and other alms) would be of benefit to the dead. This can be found in Madagascar to this very day. Many of the people who worship in the traditional way describe visions of their ancestors appearing to them and asking for the *famadihana* service of re-burial previously describe in this book. While relief from purgatory is not the goal in the Malagasy context, the situation is very similar in the sense that the ancestors are seeking comfort in the afterlife. Moreover, in each situation repercussions occur if the spirits or ancestor's requests are not carried out. Haunting is the result of failing to acknowledging the wishes of the spirits or ancestors.

This section of the Smalcald Articles also mentions diabolical possession. When describing the abominations brought on by the Mass, Luther addresses the reason behind these deceptions. He writes:

> They do so simply because the devil has possessed the pope to praise and approve of these practices in order that great multitudes of people may turn aside from Christ to their own merits and (what is worst of all) become idolaters.[4]

In Article IV on the Papacy, Luther describes standing before the Pope and standing before Satan as one in the same. He writes:

> In the council, we shall not stand before the emperor or the secular authority, as at Augsburg, where we responded to a gracious summons and were given a kindly hearing, but we shall stand before the pope and the devil himself, who does not intend to give us a hearing but only damn, murder, and drive us to idolatry.[5]

The work of the devil is to bring idolatry into the life of God's people. He does this through the work of the Roman pontiff and pagan worship. He knows how to lead Christians away from Christ and what best to say to bring doubt.

---

[4] SA Part 2, Article 2, 19.

[5] SA Part 2, Article 4, 16.

Martin Luther's Large Catechism

His purpose is to make us scorn and despise both the Word and the works of God, to tear us away from faith, hope, and love; to draw us into unbelief, false security, and stubbornness, or, on the contrary, to drive us to despair, atheism, blasphemy, and countless other abominable sins.

—Martin Luther

The Large Catechism contains many references to the work of the devil. Luther's Large Catechism mentions the devil eighty-four times. We will focus our attention on Luther's explanation of The Lord's Prayer.[6] As one might assume, petitions six and seven have the greatest references to the work of the devil.

Petition six of the Lord's Prayer looks to the cause of all temptation. Luther identifies three: the flesh, the world, and the devil.[7] The flesh is identified with the old Adam that all people continue to carry within them. Luther identifies the old Adam as that within humanity, which leads to "unchastity, laziness, gluttony and drunkenness, greed, and deceit, into fraud and deception against our neighbor . . ."[8] The world contains many people of the flesh that carry their sins into our lives. Finally, there is Satan. Of him, Luther writes:

> His purpose is to make us scorn and despise both the Word and the works of God, to tear us away from faith, hope, and love; to draw us into unbelief, false security, and stubbornness, or, on the contrary, to drive us to despair, atheism, blasphemy, and countless other abominable sins. These are the snares and nets; indeed, they are the real "flaming darts" which are venomously shot into our hearts, not by flesh and blood, but by the devil.

---

[6] Prayer was a type of exorcism for Luther. See Thomas Meigs, "Pastoral Care Methods and Demonology in Selected Writings," *Pastoral Psychology and Christian Education* 5, no. 3 (Fall 1977): 235.

[7] LC 6th Petition, 101–102.

[8] LC 6th Petition, 102.

These are the great, grievous perils and temptations which every Christian must bear, even if they come one by one. As long as we remain in this vile life in which we are attacked, hunted, and harried on all sides, we are constrained to cry out and pray every hour that God may not allow us to become faint and weary and to fall back to sin, shame, and unbelief. Otherwise, it is impossible to overcome even the least temptations.[9]

No one is a stranger to temptation. We are all sinners. Temptation is always a part of our lives, and it will be until that day when Christ Jesus frees us from this world of death, but what in the meantime while we live in the corruption of the flesh? What is Luther's advice on how we should stand against these temptations? He writes:

Accordingly, we Christians must be armed and prepared for incessant attacks. Then we shall not go about securely and heedlessly as if the devil were far from us but shall at all times expect his blows and parry them.[10]

The arming that Luther describes is in the Lord's Prayer. However, the Lord's Prayer is not a magical incantation that can free us from temptation by merely speaking the words. The object of the prayer, namely Jesus, is our protector. By remembering this, we will pray with full confidence in our Lord who has promised to protect us in all times, both good and bad. Now that Luther has provided the proper understanding of prayer, he focus on the Lord's Prayer as one of the greatest weapons given to the believer for protection against the flesh, the world, and the devil. Luther writes:

At such times, your only hope or comfort is to take refuge in the Lord's Prayer and to appeal to God from your heart, "Dear Father, Thou hast commanded me to pray; let me not fall because of temptation." Then you will see temptation cease and eventually admit defeat. Otherwise, if you attempt to help yourself by your own thoughts and counsels you will

---

[9] LC 6th Petition, 104–105.

[10] LC 6th Petition, 109.

only make the matter worse and give the devil a better opening . . . Prayer can resist him and drive him back.[11]

While temptation remains threefold (flesh, world, and devil), it is the devil who uses the first two means of temptation to his advantage. Prayer, specifically the Lord's Prayer, is a weapon against the devil. Therefore, the next petition rightfully declares, "but deliver us from evil."

In his opening remarks to the Seventh Petition, Luther reminds his readers that this petition of the prayer is more accurately translated from the Greek as "deliver us from the evil one." He writes:

> The petition seems to be speaking of the devil as the sum of all evil in order that the entire substance of our prayer may direct against our arch-enemy. It is he who obstructs everything that we pray for: God's name or glory, God's kingdom and will, our daily bread, a good and cheerful conscience, etc.[12]

Luther also understands the evil of the world. The world remains in the bondage of the devil and sin reigns in the world. Therefore, this petition is also acceptable in the more general form of "deliver us from evil." Luther writes:

> This petition includes all the evil that may befall us under the devil's kingdom: poverty, shame, death, and, in short, all the tragic misery and heartache of which there is so incalculably much on earth.[13]

Christ has delivered us from the devil, and he continues to do so each day. One of the most powerful delivery mechanisms God provides for his people is Holy Baptism. In the Large Catechism, Luther understands deliverance and victory over the devil to come through the gift of Holy Baptism. Baptism is the place where God frees people from the kingdom of Satan and moves them into the Kingdom of God.[14]

---

[11] LC 6th Petition, 110–111.

[12] LC 6th Petition, 113.

[13] LC 6th Petition, 115.

[14] Chemnitz clarifies Luther's thoughts on this issue. He writes, "For some indeed claim that the words sound as if the infants had been possessed [by the devil]. We

MARTIN LUTHER
ON DEMONICAL POSSESSION AND SATAN

The first thing you and your congregation ought to do is this: Pray fervently and oppose Satan with your faith, no matter how stubbornly he resists.

—Martin Luther

Luther fully accepted that Satan remains active in the world. He maintained an exorcism in his baptismal rite and wrote many times about the harassments he had received from the devil and his demons. Some of the most helpful insights into Luther's understanding of diabolical possession are demonstrated in the letters he writes to comfort various people. Theodore Tappert has edited a work, which identifies many of these letters, in a book titled *Letters of Spiritual Council.*

MARTIN LUTHER'S LETTERS OF SPIRITUAL COUNCIL

Luther is depicted as a man who found the devil everywhere. Tappert urgently desires to squash this myth early in his book.[15] It is true that Luther understood the devil to be an adversary who was always causing both spiritual and physical harm to humanity; Luther also understood the corruption that sin had brought upon God's creation. Tappert writes:

It was commonly believed that sickness could be induced by the practice of black magic. In a sermon that he preached in

---

surely know that infants are not physically filled with the blessing of God. We also know in turn from the Word of God that it is much sadder and more perilous, that, banished from the kingdom of heaven because of sin, they are held as spiritual captives under the kingdom and power of darkness, from which they cannot be set free by the power of any creature. But God the Father by His divine power, for the sake of the Son, sets them free through the Holy Spirit in Baptism. Therefore, not without weighty reason, exorcism was both received in ancient times and retained by Luther, provided the liberty of which we have spoken, remain for the church." Martin Chemnitz, *Loci Theologici*, trans. Jacob A. O. Preus (St. Louis: Concordia, 1989), 729.

[15] Theodore G. Tappert, ed., *Luther: Letters of Spiritual Counsel (Library of Christian Classics)* (New York: Westminster John Knox Press, 2006), 16.

1529, Luther referred in passing to sickness caused by sorcerers, but as a rule he traced disease to natural causes—not, to be sure, without reference to Satan's activity behind these natural causes.[16]

Luther understood very well that some of the afflictions presented to him for counsel had spiritual causes while others had physical causes, and at other times both may be encountered simultaneously.[17]

Tappert records at least six significant letters written by Luther that had the work of Satan as a primary cause of the noted affliction.[18] Two of these letters deal directly with what appears to be demonic possession. Three of the letters focus on a physical or mental phenomenon, which was believed to have Satan as the underlying cause. The final letter comes from a time of epidemic. It contains an intriguing perspective on how the devil uses fear and physical affliction to gain control over his victims.

DEMONIC POSSESSION—LETTER TO BERNARD WURZELMANN (1535)

In this first letter, we see Luther as he addresses a situation in which a woman is possessed by the devil. Luther's advice follows:

> The first thing you and your congregation ought to do is this: Pray fervently and oppose Satan with your faith, no matter how stubbornly he resists. About ten years ago, we had an experience in this neighborhood with a very wicked demon, but we succeeded in subduing him by perseverance and by unceasing prayer and unquestioning faith. The same will happen among you if you continue in Christ's name to despise that derisive and arrogant spirit and do not cease praying. By this means I have restrained many similar spirits in different places, for the prayers of the Church prevail at last.[19]

---

[16] Tappert, *Luther*, 16

[17] Tappert, *Luther*, 18.

[18] Osjord describes the different understandings of exorcism found between the Lutherans and the Reformed traditions. See Hans Naegeil Osjord, *Possession & Exorcism* (Oregon: New Frontiers Center, 1988), 53.

[19] Tappert, *Luther*, 42.

Two significant points stand out in this letter. First, Luther portrays himself as one who has fought Satan and his demons many times in the past as they took possession of other individuals. He says that he has, "restrained many similar spirits in different places." Luther is well-known as an exorcist during his time.[20] However, Luther's understanding of exorcism was hugely different from his Roman Catholic counterparts. We have all seen movies such as *The Exorcist* depicting the Roman Catholic priest fighting the demons as he reads the Roman Ritual of Exorcism. He speaks the words written on the page and follows its instructions by casting holy water on the demon apparently causing it great distress. However, Luther had no room for such foolishness. When writing on another occasion, Luther specifically warns pastors against using the Roman Rite of Exorcism.[21] The second point that comes from the letter is that the Church and prayer are the primary ways Luther advises Wurzelmann to deal with this case of possession. The church is the place where the faithful gather around the Word of Jesus and the Holy Sacraments. Through the means of Word and Sacrament, Jesus has promised to be present as a loving protector who pours out His forgiveness upon our sin-ridden bodies and souls. In the presence of Jesus, Satan cannot stand. Moreover, it is in the Divine Service of the Church where we meet as the people of God with our combined petitions. We pray, "Our Father . . ." as the collective body of Christ on this Earth, and Jesus promises to hear and answer our prayers.

Luther adds one additional warning to Wurzelmann. Luther writes:

> The second thing is this: Carefully investigate whether that woman might be practicing some fraud by means of which all of you could be made objects of ridicule. In my own experience (apart from what I have read in books) I have

---

[20] Osjord, *Possession & Exorcism*, 3.

[21] Here Luther is speaking of the medieval rites. The introduction to the English translation of the Roman Ritual, agrees with Luther that the medieval rite was loaded with, "practices that were superstitious to an extreme." The introduction goes on to admit that many medieval magical practices have been introduced into the Roman Ritual. See Philip T. Weller, trans., *The Roman Ritual: Complete Edition* (Milwaukee: Bruce Publishing, 1964), 638

encountered such frauds, and afterward I reproached myself for my simplicity.[22]

Luther knows extremely well that many times what appears to be possession may be something entirely different, maybe someone is not being truthful and are simply attempting to bring about a fraud.

DEMONIC POSSESSION—LETTER TO ANDREW EBERT (1536)

In this letter, Luther addresses a situation in which a young girl is possessed. Tappert's introduction tells us that this young girl had already undergone a failed exorcism at the hands of a Roman Catholic priest. Luther's instructions to Ebert are as follows:

> We must first pray earnestly for the girl who is compelled to suffer such things on our account. In the second place, this spirit must in turn be ridiculed and derided, but he must not be attacked with any exorcisms or serious measures, for he laughs at all these things with diabolical scorn. We persevere in our prayer for the girl and our contempt of the devil until finally, Christ permitting, he lets her alone.[23]

Luther had no use for the Roman Catholic exorcism rituals. Indeed, he earnestly spoke against using them. Instead, Luther thought it necessary to both pray earnestly for Christ's action and to ridicule the demons into leaving their host. There are two things at work in Luther's words. First, Luther understands that the only one who can drive Satan or his demons out of a person is Jesus. Luther was an experienced student of Holy Scripture, and he recognized that man does not have the power nor is this power found in wordy rituals to dislodge Satan. Jesus is the only true exorcist. The second point Luther wishes to make is that Satan can many times be vanquished by simply attacking his pride. Ridicule is not something Satan stands by and accepts. He desires to bring fear and take control; however, ridicule can cause him to flee.

Many of the Malagasy exorcists would agree with this point. A number of their exorcists continually ridicule a demon while at the same time, they avoid wordy exorcism rituals. They too understand only Jesus can bring about a cure to the possessed. Therefore, the

---

[22] Tappert, *Luther*, 43.

[23] Tappert, *Luther*, 44.

only ritual used is the invocation of Jesus' name was the command to depart. This follows remarkably closely to what Luther recommends in these letters.

SATAN AND PHYSICAL AFFLICTION—TABLE TALK RECORDED BY ANTHONY LAUTERBACH (1538)

In this letter, Luther deals with the differences between physical causes and demonic causes of disease. His advice will do us all good to consider. For far too long the Church has simply turned cases of mental disorders and other afflictions over to the medical establishment without much more than a passing prayer for health and recovery. If we are honest with ourselves, we must admit this to be true. Pastors include those who face illness and disease in public prayers or at the bedside of the afflicted, but how often do they honestly expect a miraculous recovery? How often do they consider that this affliction is demonically imposed? No, doubt such talk is causing many who read this to feel a bit uncomfortable. You might be thinking, "This is just not the way Lutherans talk." Well, if this describes you, then just wait: this is exactly the way Luther will address the problem in his letter. Lauterbach records Luther:

> Physicians observe only the natural causes of illness and try to counteract these by means of their remedies. They do well to do this. But they do not understand that Satan is sometimes the instigator of the material cause of the disease; he can alter the causes and diseases at once, and he can turn a fever into chills and health into illness. To deal with Satan there must be a higher medicine, namely, faith and prayer.[24]

Science and natural causes should not be our answer for every affliction. Physicians are gifts of God and workers of his healing, but many times, there are spiritual causes behind physical problems. We would do well to remember this scriptural teaching when dealing with the sick and afflicted.

DEMONIC SUICIDE—LETTER TO WIDOW MARGARET (1528)

If the previous letter caused you discomfort, this next one may be even more difficult to accept. Too many of us have been affected by

---

[24] Tappert, *Luther*, 46.

the unexpected death of a loved one, but suicide is one of the most difficult of actions to understand. We say things like, "what a waste" or "why would they do this?" Christians struggle over the salvation of those who inflicted such injury and death upon themselves. While many times suicide is the result of chemical changes in the brain that can be treated by modern medicine, sometimes there seems to be no indication of these things. At other times, suicide might be the ultimate act of unbelief; such acts end in condemnation by God. However, Luther recognizes another cause of suicide that many within our time have passed over.

In this letter, Luther writes to a widow who has recently lost her husband to suicide. Luther was ahead of his time on these matters. He understood that, on many occasions, the individual who commits suicide does not freely choose to do so, but may be driven to death by the assaults of the devil. He comforts the widow as he writes:

> That your husband inflicted injury upon himself may be explained by the devil's power over our members. He may have directed your husband's hand even against his will. For if your husband had done what he did of his own free will, he would surely not have come to himself and turned to Christ with such a confession of faith. How often the devil breaks arms, legs, backs, and all members! He can be master of the body and its members against our will.[25]

From this letter, it appears that Luther understands the suicidal man to be a Christian. Therefore, one could conclude from this letter that Luther accepted the idea that Christians may be subject to possession by demons. He uses the terminology of Satan directing the hand of the man. Luther could mean that Satan planted the thought or suggestion into the man's mind to kill himself, but it could just as well mean that Satan did the deed through the possession of the man's literal "hands." Should not the Church at least consider such things? How many deaths could be prevented by recognizing the work of Satan and casting it away by the name of Jesus? I will leave this for you to consider as we move on to Luther's next topic, depression.

---

[25] Tappert, *Luther*, 59.

DEMONIC DEPRESSION—LETTER TO JEROME WELLER (1530)

Just as Satan can bring about physical affliction to the body, and even direct the will of man, in this letter Luther describes how Satan can assault the mind by bringing on depression. He writes:

> My dear Jerome: You must believe that this temptation of yours is of the devil, who vexes you so because you believe in Christ.[26]

Once again, Luther has identified this individual as a faithful Christian who is undergoing assault by the devil. Depression is a problem that has been running rampant in the western world. However, it is intriguing that depression is rarely a significant problem in some of the most difficult parts of the world. There are places where starvation and disaster constantly bombard the people, yet an exceptionally low number of cases of depression are found when compared with places like the United States and Europe. Why is this? Could it be that most of these places still recognize the devil and spirits as being a possible cause of affliction and direct their prayers to Jesus for liberation? If we were to ask our African or Malagasy friends, they would answer in the affirmative. One African pastor remarked, "How can you fight a war if you forget that your enemies are hiding outside your camp in the bush? As soon as you walked outside you would be slaughtered." Yet, for far too many Christians this is how they proceed; they walk around without noticing the activities of the evil one in their midst and, as a result, fall prey to his affliction and death. Listen, as Luther now gives his advice to the faithful Jerome who is enduring fits of depression:

> Whenever this temptation comes to you, avoid entering upon disputation with the devil and do not allow yourself to dwell on those deadly thoughts, for to do so is nothing short of yielding to the devil and letting him have his way. Try as hard as you can to despise those thoughts, which are induced by the devil. In this sort of temptation and struggle, contempt is the best and easiest method of winning over the devil. Laugh your adversary to scorn and to ask who it is with whom you are talking. By all means flee solitude, for the devil watches and lies in wait for you most of all when you are alone. The

---

[26] Tappert, *Luther*, 84.

devil is conquered by mocking and despising him, not by resisting and arguing with him.[27]

Luther suggests ridicule for a defense against satanic activity. Luther's encouragement to flee solitude is also helpful. Solitude breeds internal debate, but when the depressed person is forced into a group it becomes necessary to interact with others rather than to hide away. If Satan can bring depression upon the saints and convince them to stay away from others, he has won a significant victory. Yet, so often, he uses fear to keep us away from others. The next letter is directed against the fear and assault brought by Satan.

DEMONIC FEAR AND ASSAULT—LETTER TO JOHN HESS (1527)

Luther lived in a time of plagues and diseases. Any student of medieval history has read of the terrible plagues of that time. This final letter comes from a time of plague. John Hess is asking Luther if the clergy should flee the areas of the plague or stay and serve their people. Such questions are not foreign to our times. Not only do we continue to face diseases, but also, we must contend with the possibility of biological warfare, the radiation from dirty bombs and the possibility of nuclear war. How should those who are called to provide pastoral care for these individuals react to the fears they will no doubt encounter because of such service? Luther's thoughts on this problem remain as timely and necessary for us as they were for the people of his day. The letter we are about to review is quite lengthy. Therefore, only the portion pertaining to fear and affliction caused by the devil, and Luther's response on how to combat this assault are quoted in this section. As to Satan's ability to bring fear and affliction, Luther writes:

> The devil is so very evil that he not only tries constantly to kill and murder but also gives vent to his spleen by making us fearful, afraid, and timid about death in order that death might appear to us to be the worst possible thing, that we might have neither rest nor peace in this life, and that we might despair our life. In this way he tries to bring it about that we despair of God, become unwilling and unprepared to die, become so enveloped in the dark clouds of fear and worry

---

[27] Tappert, *Luther*, 85.

that we forget and lose sight of Christ, our light and life, forsake our neighbor in his need and so sin against man and God. This is the devil's desire and purpose. Because we know that such fear and terror are the devil's game, we should be more unwilling to be affected by it, gather up our courage in defiance of him and to vex him, and throw off his terror and cast it back at him.[28]

One should stay and care for those who are in need even if there is a great risk to one's own life. Yet, the question remains how can one overcome the fear of such unknown? Luther is clear:

We should defend ourselves with such weapons and say: "Away with you and your fears, devil!" Because it will vex you, I shall defy you by going at once to my sick neighbor to help him. I shall pay no attention to you [devil] but shall attack you on two points. The first is that I know for certain that this work is pleasing to God and all the angels when I do it in obedience to his will and divine service . . . The other point on which to attack the devil is the sure promise of God with which he comforts all those who consider the poor and needy.[29]

Luther directs those who fear to look upon the promises and the accomplishments of Jesus. Luther's answer is Scripture's answer. It is Jesus' answer to the despairing John the Baptist:

Go and tell John what you hear and see: the blind receive their sight and the lame walk, lepers are cleansed and the deaf hear, and the dead are raised up, and the poor have good news preached to them. And blessed is the one who is not offended by Me.[30]

Jesus has done everything necessary for the needy already, upon the cross. Justification is God's answer for all people. Moreover, Luther understands that through justification, people are set free to live their lives for the benefit of others. Luther's answer to Hess is to stand firm and do not fear. The devil may be powerful and a great

---

[28] Tappert, *Luther*, 237.

[29] Tappert, *Luther*, 238.

[30] Matthew 11:4–6; Luke 7:22–23.

adversary, but before the Word of God, he is nothing to be feared. How can Luther be so bold as to say such things? He recognizes the benefit of his Baptism and the promises of God through the water and the word. In Baptism, Satan is defeated in the individual just as he was defeated upon the cross. For that is what Baptism does—it connects us to the cross and the resurrection of our victorious Lord and Savior. Therefore, it is necessary for us to review Luther's baptismal liturgies for additional clarification and instruction in the benefits of Holy Baptism in the fight against the trickery of the evil one.

BAPTISM AS EXORCISM; LUTHER'S BAPTISMAL RITES OF 1523 AND 1526

The 1523 Rite of Holy Baptism

Luther continued to promote the necessity of Baptism for both adults and infants. Luther wrote his first German translation of the Rite for Holy Baptism in 1523. It contained many aspects of the Roman Rite of his time, which included a series of exorcisms, although he did make some slight adjustments. The *American Edition of Luther's Works* describes the changes of 1523:

> This baptismal liturgy follows the traditional Roman rite, except that the exorcism has been abbreviated, the Creed moved from its place before the Lord's Prayer to the questions, and the collect "*Deus patrum nostrorum*" (God of our Fathers) has been replaced by the so-called "flood prayer" (*Sintflutgebet*).[31]

Luther did not care for the extensive prayers and rubrics of the Roman Rite of exorcism, but he continues to retain the exorcisms. The Rite begins with the officiant blowing three times under the child's eyes and saying, "Depart thou unclean spirit and give room to the Holy Spirit."[32] Following the first of the exorcisms, the sign of the cross is then marked upon the forehead and the heart of the baptized. Satan is cast out, and the person is marked as one of God's own. The

---

[31] Martin Luther, *Luther's Works American Edition (Liturgy and Hymns AE 53)*, ed. Helmut T. Lehmann, trans. Paul Zeller Strodach, 55 vols. (New York: Augsburg Fortress, 1965), 95.

[32] AE 53:96.

following prayer is a commentary of the exorcism previously administered:

> O Almighty eternal God, Father of our Lord Jesus Christ, look upon N., thy servant whom thou hast called to instruction in the faith, drive away from him all blindness of his heart, break all the snares of the devil with which he is bound, open him, Lord, the door of thy grace: So that marked with the sign of thy wisdom he may be freed of the stench of all evil lust and serve thee joyfully according to the sweet savor of thy commandments in thy church and grow daily and be made meet to come to the grace of thy baptism to receive the balm of life; through Christ our Lord. Amen.[33]

Salt is offered as the prayers continue:

> Therefore, thou miserable devil, acknowledge thy judgment and give glory to the true and living God, give glory to his Son Jesus Christ and to the Holy Ghost, and depart from N., his servant; for God and the Lord Jesus Christ has of his goodness called him to his holy grace and blessing, and to the fountain of baptism so that thou mayest never dare to disturb this sign of the holy cross + which we make on his forehead; through him who cometh again to judge . . . etc.

> So harken now, thou miserable devil, adjured by the name of the eternal God and our Savior Jesus Christ, and depart trembling and groaning, conquered together with thy hatred so that thou shall have nothing to do with the servant of God who now seeks that which is heavenly and renounces thee and thy world, and shall live in blessed immortality. Give glory therefore now to the Holy Ghost who cometh and descendeth from the loftiest castle of heaven in order to destroy thy deceit and treachery, and having cleansed the heart with divine fountain, to make it ready, a holy temple and dwelling of God, freed from all guilt of former sin, may always give thanks to the eternal God and praise his name forever and ever. Amen.[34]

---

[33] AE 53:96.

[34] AE 53:98.

In this prayer, the devil is understood to be weak and pitiful ("depart trembling and groaning, conquered together with thy hatred"). The devil must depart because he has no authority to stay. The rite continues:

> I adjure thee, thou unclean spirit, by the name of the Father +
> and the Son + and the Holy Ghost + that thou come out of
> and depart from this servant of God, N., for he commands
> thee, thou miserable one, he who walked upon the sea and
> stretched forth his hand to sinking Peter.[35]

Luther uses the divine name of God and then demands the devil to depart. There is no power in the officiant, the power and the command to depart originates in Jesus. The devil is the "miserable one" while Jesus is the "powerful one" who has, "walked upon the sea and stretched forth his hand to sinking Peter."

The rite contains one final exorcism. It is simple in form and command, "But thou, devil, flee; for God's judgment cometh speedily."[36] The devil is ridiculed and told, "You better get going devil, Jesus is coming, and you do not want to be here when he arrives." Following this, the renunciation of Satan takes place and the baptismal liturgy continues until the actual Baptism.

Luther adds some commentary following his baptismal rite, which reminds all of the significance of Baptism for the child of God. In this commentary, Luther warns his readers:

> Remember, therefore, that it is no joke to take sides against
> the devil and not only to drive him away from the little child,
> but also to burden the child with such a mighty and lifelong
> enemy.[37]

This is a reminder to all the baptized, Satan is "the old evil foe," who seeks to devour those who carry the Lord's name.[38] This world is engaged in a spiritual battle even after Jesus' defeat of Satan upon the cross.[39] Baptism into the Holy Name of the Triune God brings one to

---

[35] AE 53:98.

[36] AE 53:99.

[37] AE 53:102.

[38] 1 Peter 5:8.

[39] Ephesians 6:12.

the front of the battle lines. However, the baptized must not fear, because their foe has already been defeated in Christ Jesus.

The 1526 Rite of Holy Baptism

Luther's baptismal liturgy underwent modifications in 1526. Ulrich S. Leupold describes the changes:

> Omitted was the exsufflation, the first of the two exorcisms, the prayer after the exorcism, the salutation before the Gospel, the *Ephphatha*, the two anointing's before and after baptism, and the placing of the lighted candle in the child's hands.[40]

Leupold has made a slight error in his statement. The 1526 rite removes the final exorcism, not the first. Luther strikes the words, "But thou, devil, flee; for God's judgment cometh speedily."[41] Nevertheless, Luther continued to recognize the immense power and promise of God in the life of the baptized.

Both of these baptismal liturgies demonstrate the importance and seriousness Luther placed upon the necessity of exorcism in its proper state. Jesus was doing the work. He was casting out the devil in Holy Baptism just as He had done in all of the exorcisms found in Holy Scripture.

This chapter has demonstrated that the reality of Satan, the demonic and diabolical possession remains prominent throughout reformation thought. While at times modernism and rationalism have lessened this truth, it nevertheless has remained a historical Christian teaching. The next section provides a connecting point between Luther and modern theologians, all of whom have continued to write and teach the necessity of recognizing Satan and his attempts to draw the people of God back into captivity.

---

[40] AE 53:106.

[41] AE 53:99.

RECENT ANSWERS FROM THE CHURCH

It is the preacher's duty to visit those members of his congregation who, while not physically ill, have been visited by some other severe misfortune or find themselves in special spiritual danger and distress; who are in danger of falling away to a false religion; who stand in severe temptations by their own hearts. The world, and the devil; who are physically possessed by Satan; and the like.

—C. F. W. Walther

C. F. W. WALTHER (1811–1887)

Pastoral Theology

C. F. W. Walther, the first president of The Lutheran Church—Missouri Synod describes the vocation and duty of Lutheran pastors in such a way that all should be reminded of their important callings:

> The God-given (*theodotos*) practical ability of the soul, acquired (*acquisitus*) through certain auxiliary means, by virtue of which a minister of the church is enabled to carry out all his functions as such in a valid (*rato*) and legitimate (*legitime*) way, to the glory of God, for the salvation of his listeners and himself.[42]

Pastoral theology is "not merely a body of knowledge, but rather a disposition or condition of the soul, a preparation to deal with the object."[43] Jesus calls pastors and equips them with His Word and Sacrament. They are to deliver forgiveness and comfort into the lives of Christ's people.

In chapter thirty-four of his book, *The Pastoral Care of the Troubled*, Walther talks of the problem of spiritual warfare. He writes:

> It is the preacher's duty to visit those members of his congregation who, while not physically ill, have been visited

---

[42] C. F. W. Walther, *Walther's Pastorale, that is, American Lutheran Pastoral Theology*, trans. John M. Dickamer (New Haven, MO: Lutheran News, 1995), 8.

[43] Walther, *Walther's Pastorale*, 8.

by some other severe misfortune or find themselves in special spiritual danger and distress; who are in danger of falling away to a false religion; who stand in severe temptations by their own hearts. The world, and the devil (with doubts about divine truth, with despair, with blasphemous and suicidal thoughts); who are involved in dangerous trials; who come to be seriously suspected of a severe crime or have already been thrown into prison; who have fallen into melancholy (depression), insanity, etc.; who are physically possessed by Satan; and the like.[44]

The remainder of the chapter deals with the problem of physical possession. Walther, following J. W. Baier, demonstrates that physical possession is a reality with which the pastor must occasionally come in contact. Moreover, Walther reminds his readers that God allows possession to occur. This too is a difficult concept for most of us to understand or accept, but Walther presents it to his readers with exceptional clarity:

For although the purpose of this possession from Satan's side is harm and corruption, in part to the person himself, in part to other people; yet from God's side, who permits it and is thereby either visiting severe sins (despising God's Word, carnal security, blasphemies, conspiracy with the devil) with his serious judgment or is rebuking and testing devout persons through physical chastening, the purpose is the revelation of His power, righteousness, and goodness; and repentance, faith, and salvation of people, if not the possessed person himself, at least of others, namely the eye and ear witnesses.[45]

There is no dualism found in Walther's theology. Satan does not have any power except that which has been granted to him by God. Even the very act of demoniacal possession only occurs with God's command or, at minimum, His consent. Indeed, God does not cause evil to occur, but He does bring good through it.[46]

---

[44] Walther, *Walther's Pastorale*, 214.

[45] Walther, *Walther's Pastorale*, 215.

[46] Romans 8:28.

So how are we to recognize demonic-possession? Walther quotes an early Lutheran theologian by the name of Quenstedt as to the "marks of possession:"

> The knowledge of foreign languages as well as arts and sciences which the possessed persons have never before learned and if they are freed, no longer know;
>
> Knowing and stating things which are hidden, which have happened elsewhere, in very distant regions, or which are in the future;
>
> Superhuman or supernatural power and strength;
>
> The exact reproduction of the voices of birds, sheep, cattle, etc., without the disposition of the organs necessary for it;
>
> Obscenity in speech;
>
> Monstrosity in gestures;
>
> Horrifying screaming (Mark 5:5);
>
> Blasphemy toward God and scorn for the neighbor;
>
> Fury and violence against one's own body and against the others watching (Matthew 8:26; 17:15; Mark 5:5; Acts 19:16).[47]

After quoting this extensive list, Walther notes that not all of these symptoms are necessary, any one of them might represent diabolical possession.[48]

---

[47] Walther, *Walther's Pastorale*, 215.

[48] The list of symptoms proposed by Lutheran theologians is in line with that offered by some within modern psychology. The modern list includes physical, psychological, and spiritual indicators. They are included here for comparison: "Physical Indicators: 1. The presence of a different voice ... particularly one proclaiming fear or hatred; 2. Convulsions occur in the individual when the evil spirit is exorcized; 3. Occurrences of unwanted, forced behavior; 4. Anesthesia to pain; 5. Super human strength; 6. Levitation is observed; 7. Poltergeist phenomenon observed. Psychological Indicators: 1. Appearances of a separate personality; 2. Individual subjectively experiences the entity as not being part of himself; 3. Individual hears an internal voice that does not have an associated personality; 4. Individual experiences confusion or clouding of consciousness; 5. Sudden and complete relief is experienced after exorcism; 6. No benefit from therapy or medication; 7. Addictive patterns of behavior; 8. Telepathy, clairvoyance of other

Walther then teaches his students that only God can drive out the devil. Man is not capable of this feat. He quotes Luther as saying:

> We cannot now and should not drive out the devils with certain ceremonies and words as previously the prophets, Christ, and the apostles did. We should pray in the name of Jesus Christ and seriously admonish the church to pray that dear God and the Father of our Lord and Savior Jesus Christ will free the possessed person through His mercy ... otherwise we cannot drive out evil spirits and also do not have the power to do it. . . . The power of God must do it, and one must risk his life, for the devil will make it terrifying enough for him.[49]

Walther and Luther condemn the old Roman Catholic understanding of exorcism that required extensive rites for the priest to perform to cast out the devil. This becomes clearer as Walther proceeds. Walther proceeds to address the abuses found within the Roman Catholic Church and its leader the Pope.[50] Walther understands the successes of the Roman exorcist to be a "sham" which Satan uses to distract people from trust and faith in God.

What does Walther recommend for Christians who have been possessed? At first, this question might be a problem for the reader. Lutheran theologians have in general accepted the possibility of the possession of Christians by evil spirits. The list includes a number of Lutheran theologians, such as, Walther,[51] Baier,[52] Quenstedt,[53] Balduin,[54] and Fecht,[55] but should not be limited exclusively to them.

---

paranormal knowledge is present; speaks fluently and/or understands a previously unknown language. Spiritual Indicators: 1. Revulsion to the name of Jesus, Christian symbols and/or prayer; 2. Arrogant attitude; 3. Stark change in moral character; 4. Lack of spiritual growth in Christians; 5. Prior occult involvement." See, Christopher H. Rosik, "When Discernment Fails: The Case for Outcome Studies on Exorcism," *Journal of Psychology and Theology* 25, no. 3 (1997): 356. Dr. Hans Naegeil Osjord also provides another view from modern psychology; see Hans Naegeil Osjord, *Possession & Exorcism,* 176.

[49] Walther, *Walther's Pastorale*, 216.

[50] Walther, *Walther's Pastorale*, 217.

[51] Carl Ferdinand Wilhelm Walther (1811–1887). First President of the Missouri Synod: 1847–1850 & 1864–1878. "He began as the editor of *Der Lutheraner* in 1844 and of *Lehre und Wehre* in 1855. He worked on both of these publications until his death. Walther authored several books, including *Die Stimme unserer Kirche in der*

For the Christian afflicted with demon-possession, Walther recommends the writings of Balduin and Fecht, both who propose the frequent reception of the Lord's Supper and Holy Absolution during the "lucid hours" between attacks.[56] Once again, Walther reminds his readers that where Jesus stands, the devil must flee. In the gift of the Lord's Supper, Jesus has promised to be present in the very unique way of His body and blood for the forgiveness of sins. Where sin is forgiven, Satan is emptied of his power and loses all hope of victory.

The Proper Distinction Between Law and Gospel

Walther understood the activity of Satan to be an ongoing problem plaguing the Church at all times. Satan's activity does not subside just because one becomes a Christian. Indeed, Scripture brings even greater warning to us who carry Jesus' name upon our brow. For years, The Reformed Churches, particularly those found in American Evangelicalism, have denied the possession of Christians by Satan so much so that many pastors, at great harm to the faithful, overlook such a possibility. Walther, following Luther, knew that such logic was severely misleading and harmful for Christians. In his *Pastorale*, he expressed his acceptance of the possession of baptized believers. In *The Proper Distinction Between Law and Gospel*, Walther describes a situation he experienced with a demon-possessed girl:

Frage von Kirche und Amt (1852), *Die rechte Gestalt einer vom Staate unabhaengigen ev.-luth. Ortsgemeinde* (1863), *Die ev.-luth. Kirche die wahre sichtbare Kirche Gottes auf Erden* (1867), *Amerikanisch-Lutherische Pastoraltheologie* (1872), *Brosamen* (1876), and *Der Gnadenwahlslehrstreit* (1881). After his death, his lectures on *Die rechte Unterscheidung von Gesetz und Evangelium* were published (1897)." "C. F. W. Walther," Concordia Historical Institute: Department of Archives and History, LCMS, Summary, http://chi.lcms.org/presidents/pres_walther.htm (accessed July 5, 2010).

[52] Johann Wilhelm Baier (1657–1695), Lutheran professor and rector at Jena and Halle. His chief work was *Compendium Theologiae Positivae.*

[53] Johannes Andreas Quenstedt (1617–1688), Lutheran professor of Wittenberg, Germany, was the foremost leader of orthodox Lutheranism.

[54] Friedrich Balduin (1575–1627), Lutheran professor of Wittenberg, Germany.

[55] Johannes Fecht (1636–1716), Lutheran theologian and opponent of pietism.

[56] Walther, *Walther's Pastorale*, 217.

I have had to treat spiritually a girl, who even uttered thoughts of this kind, but at the same time fell on the ground, weeping and moaning to be delivered from her affliction by God. She did not come to rest until she realized that it was not she uttering those thoughts. Satan had taken possession of her lips. Of course, Modernists, who deny such power of the devil, call this explanation a superstitious notion.[57]

Walther's last statement is significant for our purposes for two reasons. First, he acknowledges that demoniacal possession continues to occur in modern day. Second, he points out that many in the modern day world will not accept this truth. Such ideas, we will see, are not limited to Walther. One of the greatest systematic writers of the Lutheran Church also accepted such possibilities. We will now turn our attention to Francis Pieper.

FRANCIS PIEPER (1852–1931)

Also children of God may suffer this affliction; by it the devil, under God's sufferance.

—Francis Pieper

Francis Pieper was a Lutheran pastor and theologian. His life work was *Christliche Dogmatik.* Both of the current seminaries of The Lutheran Church—Missouri Synod continue to use this work as a primary systematic textbook. In the chapter dealing with *Angelology*, Pieper describes the activity of the devil. He states, "the fact that men do not know this [that they are doing the work of the devil], yes, even deny the existence of the devil, is likewise due to the operation of the devil."[58] Already early in the nineteenth century, many people were in denial of Satan and his demons' continued activity in the world.[59] Of bodily possession (*obsession corporalis*) Pieper writes:

---

[57] C. F. W. Walther, *Proper Distinction Between Law and Gospel*, trans. W. H. T. Dau (St. Louis: Concordia, 1986), 394.

[58] Francis Pieper, *Christian Dogmatics*, vol. 1. Translated by Theodore Engelder. (St. Louis: Concordia, 1957), 509.

[59] "Today's view, which dominates psychiatric literature, seeks to attribute mental illnesses, including possession, to chemical changes in the brain cells and their fluid chemistry." See Hans Naegeil Osjord, *Possession & Exorcism,* 9.

Also children of God may suffer this affliction; by it the devil, under God's sufferance, takes possession of a man by personally dwelling in him, so that the demoniac, bereft of the use of his reason and will, becomes the involuntary instrument of Satan. The human personality no longer functions; the devil in person becomes the acting subject. The demoniac is no longer responsible for his actions.[60]

Pieper clearly accepts the possibility of demoniacal possession, which includes the possession of believing Christians. Moreover, Pieper accepts that such possession cannot occur by Satan's power. God must provide His passive consent for any such case of possession as it pertains to one of His children.

THE PASTORAL THEOLOGY OF JOHN H. C. FRITZ (1874–1953) AND BEYOND[61]

For many years *Pastoral Theology* by John H. C. Fritz was the main textbook used for training Lutheran pastors. In his book, Fritz quotes Walther directly when answering the question of demoniacal possession. Yet, before doing so, he advises his readers not to ignore demoniacal possession as fiction. Fritz writes:

We have no reason to believe that cases of demonic possession were limited to the time of Christ and the Apostles, and to the early Church. Nevertheless great care must be exercised in the diagnosis, especially if demonic possession is suspected in a person who is known to be a sincere Christian, a child of God.[62]

It is significant that Fritz finds it necessary to present this material in such a way. While Walther was aware that many theologians of his time were in denial of ongoing satanic activity, he expected his readers to share his belief in demoniacal possession. However, Fritz, it appears, expected some doubt to be within the minds of his students. Already in the early years of the twentieth century, there was a movement within The Lutheran Church—Missouri Synod

---

[60] Pieper, *Christian Dogmatics*, 509.

[61] Dr. John H. C. Fritz was a professor at the Missouri Synod's seminary in St. Louis during the 1930s and '40s.

[62] John H. C. Fritz, *Pastoral Theology* (St. Louis: Concordia, 2003), 209.

toward rationalism and the denial of the realities of the devil, especially demonic possession. However, later Lutheran publications would soon almost dismiss this possibility.

In 1974, Northwestern Publishing House released a pastoral theology under the title, *The Shepherd under Christ*.[63] This book almost completely avoids the work of Satan, demonology, or demoniacal possession—so much so, that the subject matter does not even get a mention.

In 1990, a new *Pastoral Theology* that took the place of Fritz's work entered the arena of pastoral theologies. This new book was considered to be a necessity for the complexities of the day.[64] However, the book fails to address demonic possession. Instead, it focuses on mental illness and phobias. To be sure, it was necessary for pastors to learn of the advance of modern medicine and the assistance professional counseling and medications could provide for those afflicted with mental difficulties and diseases, but its shortcoming was that it no longer acknowledged the work of Satan and the demonic in some cases. As we will see, things continue to deteriorate in pastoral writings and theologies before they get better, but do not worry, they do get better. First, we must review our next sources.

Finally, in 1994, Concordia Publishing House began to correct the situation with the release of Richard C. Eyer's, *Pastoral Care Under the Cross*. In this book, Eyer brings the discussion back to life as he writes:

> Almost from the beginning of time God's reign has been disputed sovereignty, a conflict that engages us in spiritual warfare. Whether we say that people are inhabited by demons (as Jesus did), or we call them mentally ill, we are identifying a deeper reality in which sin and grace compete for the soul. Although few of us would be likely to reduce mental illness to demonology, our Lord surely is pointing us even today to

---

[63] Armin W. Schuetze and Irwin J. Habeck, *The Shepherd under Christ* (Milwaukee: Northwestern, 1974).

[64] Norbert H. Mueller and George Kraus, eds., *Pastoral Theology* (St. Louis: Concordia, 1990), 7.

> the reality of the persona of evil and its spiritual powers, which have in mind to destroy the human soul.[65]

> The understanding of ourselves as psychological beings has been helpful in modern times, but it also has had its limitations. We need to look beyond to the deeper spiritual realities. What does it mean to be spiritual beings with spiritual problems for which God offers spiritual solutions? Pastors need to acknowledge and accept psychology, but at the same time recognize the ragged-edge limits of psychology as we reach out to the mentally ill to offer them the seamless robe of Christ.[66]

Finally, Eyer moves the discussion back to the spiritual while at the same time helping pastors understand common mental illness. The next chapter of this book is reserved for the presentation of this information. For now, we continue to look toward more contemporary theologians.

The next theologian presented in this section, namely Helmut Thielicke, has some of the most informative advice on the topic of the demonic and spiritual warfare available at the time of his writing up to the time of the writing of this book.

HELMUT THIELICKE (1908–1996)

Helmut Thielicke was a Lutheran author of the twentieth century and professor of Dogmatics in Germany during WWII who underwent the persecution of Nazi Germany.

---

[65] Richard C. Eyer, *Pastoral Care Under the Cross: God in the Midst of Suffering* (St. Louis: Concordia, 1994), 116.

[66] Eyer, *Pastoral Care Under the Cross*, 117.

The Evangelical Faith

> *Unbelief undoubtedly begins with this ideological slavery to*
> *the age and rejection of all thought of the devil. "Unbelief*
> *begins with me," says the devil . . .*

—Helmut Thielicke

The Evangelical Faith is a multiple-volume work. In volume three of his book, Thielicke takes up the topic of demonology in the modern world. "How can one discuss evil without discussing the devil?"[67] Thielicke puts this question to his readers. No one during the time of Thielicke would deny that evil was in the world. World War II had made it abundantly clear for Thielicke that evil had not disappeared. Those who held a postmillennial view of Jesus' return began to change their position. Utopian ideas were inconceivable when faced with death and destruction. Thielicke had experienced evil through the affliction he received at the hands of Hitler and the Nazis. There was no doubt evil was real and inflicting serious harm upon the world. Thielicke knew that evil and the devil were inseparable. One cannot be discussed without the other. Yet, modern men, including theologians, were beginning to reject these things as superstition. Therefore, Thielicke tackles the problem of unbelief:

> Unbelief undoubtedly begins with this ideological slavery to
> the age and rejection of all thought of the devil. "Unbelief
> begins with me," says the devil . . . In spite of such pleas for
> the existence of the devil both inside and outside Christianity,
> many theologians find the theme embarrassing.[68]

Unbelief is a sign of the devil's very existence. A dead man does not know he is dead. He has been born spiritually dead and under the captivity of the devil. In Ephesians chapter two, Paul addresses this problem. He uses the Greek word for corpse (*nekrous*) to describe the pre-converted state of men.[69] Yet, Paul is not speaking about physical death. He refers to those who are literally "walking dead" people.

---

[67] Helmut Thielicke, *The Evangelical Faith*, vol. 3. Translated by Geffrey W. Bromiley. (Grand Rapids: Eerdmans, 1977), 448.

[68] Thielicke, *The Evangelical Faith*, 3:449.

[69] Ephesians 2:1.

Those who have not been made alive by the Word of God are lost in captivity and blindness of Satan. Paul writes:

> And you were dead in the trespasses and sins in which you once walked, following the course of this world, following the prince of the power of the air, the spirit that is now at work in the sons of disobedience—among whom we all once lived in the passions of our flesh, carrying out the desires of the body and the mind, and were by nature children of wrath, like the rest of mankind.[70]

Thielicke appreciates this, but many of his contemporaries do not; they have walked away from such biblical theology. Why do so many modern-day theologians refuse to accept the reality of the devil? Thielicke identifies three reasons:

1. The fear of being perceived as a simpleton by one's academic peers.

2. Recognizing that the demonic cannot be placed into scientific categories or objective terms.

3. Because evil cannot be seen by the evil just as stupidity cannot be perceived by the stupid.[71]

Thielicke is correct: the problem for unbelief lies within the individual who is in bondage to Satan. The spiritually dead cannot see the reality of the curse in which they have been bound. Therefore, those who will not accept the truth cannot accept the devil; he becomes an impossibility for them. Only an act of God can bring the truth of the untruth to light within the mind of humanity. The Scriptures are clear on this point. Paul writes about the spiritual captivity of man in various sections of his many epistles.[72] Paul understands people to be spiritually dead before the "Word of truth" comes to bring life.[73] The spiritually dead are in bondage to Satan. The whole of humanity begins in this bondage, but Christians are now in Christ rather than belonging to Satan who once controlled them. As

---

[70] Ephesians 2:1–3.

[71] Thielicke, *The Evangelical Faith*, 3:448.

[71] Thielicke, *The Evangelical Faith*, 3:449.

[72] Ephesians 1:13, 2:1–22; Colossians 3:1–14; Romans 10:17; etc.

[73] Ephesians 1:13.

was demonstrated in Part One of this book, many of the Christian converts found in the Malagasy context describe their previous lives as bondage and darkness. Yet, when in that darkness they never knew of their bondage. Therefore, the world remains in this spiritual bondage too often unaware of the existence of Satan and his demons.

Thielicke adds two additional points that require examination concerning demonic possession. The first is the impossibility of personal communication with the demonic. Thielicke writes:

> In dealing with demonic power, there is no personal communication. This is where the concept of the personal reaches its limit. On the contrary, what takes place is "possession" by an alien force and an attack on human personality. Thus, exorcism in the name of God is the only form of an encounter with demonic power and the dominion to which it aspires. We see the personality of the demonic power only indirectly and not directly.[74]

This inability to communicate apart from exorcism leads to Thielicke's second insight:

> Exorcism as liberation from possession by something alien has from this standpoint both a positive and negative side. Positively, it means filling with the Spirit of God, which drives the demonic spirit out of the victim, restores threatened identity, and brings to light the original person. Negatively, exorcism shows that power is here mobilized against power and person against person and that argument is a blunt weapon against possession and domination . . . Illuminating words are of no avail against demons. Words can even come under their power in the form of the spirit of the age. What avails against demons is only the word of command, the authority that is ascribed to Christ when he drives out demons.[75]

No exorcistic power exists apart from Jesus. Extensive rites are unnecessary; they are folly to Satan and his demons. Words cannot

---

[74] Thielicke, *The Evangelical Faith*, 3:452.

[75] Thielicke, *The Evangelical Faith*, 3:452.

affect them; demons are capable of toying with words and bringing greater deceptions upon those who speak them.

Man In God's World

One other book of Thielicke deserves mention. In his book, *Man In God's World*, Thielicke returns to the topic of the demonic. Man is in God's world, but so is Satan. Yet, men continue to deny Satan's existence, even those who accept the reality of evil. Where there is evil, there is death, destruction, disease, and the demonic. The demonic seeks to bring about sin as servitude.[76] Sin increases as the fear of evil prevails within the mind. This fear is a demonic fear that causes the individual to fall into unbelief and further into bondage.

KURT E. KOCH (1913–1987)

Koch was a noted German theologian and Lutheran pastor. He received his Doctor of Theology from Tübingen University under the direction of Adolf Koberle.[77] His dissertation was published under the title *Christian Counseling and Occultism: A Complete Guidebook to Occult Oppression and Deliverance*.[78] In this book, Koch seeks to address the problem of occult activity. Koch recognizes the value of a systematic study on the topic.[79] Therefore, he conducted a study which sought to show a correlation between mental illness and active participation with the occult. Koch concludes that occult activity could be one of the primary factors leading to the mental distress found in many throughout the world.[80] What cure does Koch suggest?

---

[76] Helmut Thielicke, *Man In God's World*. Translated by John W. Doberstein. (New York: Harper & Row, 1963), 167.

[77] John Warwick Montgomery, *Principalities and Powers: The World of the Occult* (Minneapolis: Pyramid Publications for Bethany Fellowship, 1975), 170.

[78] See also Kurt E. Koch, *Demonology Past and Present: Identifying and Overcoming Demonic Strongholds* (Grand Rapids: Kregel Publications, 2000).

[79] Kurt E. Koch, *Christian Counseling and Occultism: A Complete Guidebook to Occult Oppression and Deliverance* (Minneapolis: Kregel Publications, 1972), 25.

[80] The *Fifohazana* movement of the Lutheran Church of Madagascar accepts this explanation. The majority of the Malagasy population continues to practice the occult. Moreover, they would agree that such participation brings many psychological disturbances to the people.

It is the cure of conversion.[81] Conversion to Christianity is the only cure that brings freedom from Satan, demons, and the occult.

JOHN WARWICK MONTGOMERY

John Warwick Montgomery has been described as "the foremost living apologist for biblical Christianity."[82] Not only is Montgomery a student of law and theology, but he also has a strong interest in the occult.[83] His interest has resulted in two books pertaining to exorcism and the demonic. The first is titled *Principalities and Powers* and the second is titled *Demon Possession*. These works are serious attempts to answer the questions of the day. Both of them were prompted by the release of the movie *The Exorcist*. During this time, there was much debate occurring as to the reality of the demonic. The movie is reportedly based on real events that occurred in the life of a Lutheran boy whose name has been protected. In the interest of brevity, we will limit our examination to the book titled *Principalities and Powers*.[84] One important reminder that Montgomery puts forth in this book is that the problem of accepting the realities of the demonic are absurd because the documentation of real cases of witchcraft and demon possession are plentiful throughout the world.[85]

Later he reminds his readers that the reality of the demonic is a universal experience known to humanity and found in all cultures and parts of the world thought history. He writes:

> The problem involved in determining whether demon possession occurs and whether witchcraft works is absurdly simple. The documentation is overwhelming. Even if ninety-nine percent of all witchcraft cases are thrown out (and that

---

[81] Koch, *Christian Counseling and Occultism*, 25.

[82] John Warwick Montgomery, home page, http://www.jwm.christendom.co.uk/ (accessed December 30, 2009).

[83] Montgomery, *Principalities and Powers*, 11.

[84] John Warwick Montgomery, ed., *Demon Possession: A Medical, Historical, Anthropological, and Theological Symposium: Papers presented at the University of Notre Dame, January 8–11, 1975, under the auspices of the Christian Medical Society* (Minneapolis: Bethany Fellowship, 1975), 9. This book is a series of papers presented at a symposium labeled, "A Theological, Psychological, and Medical Symposium on the Phenomena Labeled As 'Demonic.' "

[85] Montgomery, *Principalities and Powers*, 137.

would be difficult to do), the remainder would easily establish the reality of the phenomenon.[86]

For Montgomery, there is no question as to the reality of the demonic in this world. The tragedy that he finds is that the world, especially the Church, has lost this understanding of the demonic. Montgomery agrees with Koch that much of the mental illness found within individuals is a result of occult activity.[87] However, there is no reason to fear in Montgomery's writings. He understands that the comfort and the remedy for all problems are found in Jesus. Evil and the author of evil are real and continue to affect the world, but they are defeated foes. Christ Jesus is the Lord of all and all must surrender to His power and authority. Satan and his demons are nothing when compared to the powerful name of Jesus. Where Jesus is present, Satan has already lost. Montgomery shows his Lutheran roots as he directs his readers to the power of Jesus located in the Holy Word and the Holy Sacraments.

EXEGETICAL THEOLOGIANS

We cannot stop the unbelievers from voicing their denials. We can, however, point out that the Evangelists well knew the difference between insanity and demonic possession.

—William F. Arndt

Now that we have examined Lutheran pastoral theologians, we turn to the reality of the devil and demoniacal possession as described in the writings of two well-known Lutheran exegetes, namely William F. Arndt, representing the twentieth century, and Jeffrey A. Gibbs, representing the twenty-first century. Both men have written about Satan and the reality of demonic possession in doctrinally approved commentaries of The Lutheran Church—Missouri Synod.

WILLIAM F. ARNDT (1880–1957)

Arndt provides a special section on demonic possession in his commentary on Luke's Gospel. Arndt begins with the rationale many

---

[86] Montgomery, *Principalities and Powers*, 183–184.

[87] Montgomery, *Principalities and Powers*, 138.

modern theologians have utilized to deny the reality of Satan and the demonic. He writes:

> Modern unbelief, denying that there are demons or devils, holds (1) that the demonic possession is a delusion; (2) that what the Gospels call demonic possession was simply insanity; (3) that Jesus through His personal magnetism, His "hypnotic" powers, cured persons who were unbalanced; (4) that He either shared the common superstition on the subject or otherwise accommodated Himself to erroneous beliefs of His countrymen, using their terminology.[88]

Now that Arndt has provided the arguments used against the possibility of Satan and demoniacal possession, he answers their objections:

> We cannot stop the unbelievers from voicing their denials. We can, however, point out that the Evangelists well knew the difference between insanity and demonic possession, as is indicated in the report given by Mark 3:21 of the Words of Jesus' relatives. Hence, the assumption that the Gospel writers looked upon all cases of insanity or loss of mental equilibrium as instances of devil possession is plainly false. The view that Jesus accommodated Himself to the superstition of His contemporaries, knowing well its groundlessness is not compatible with the records. His words in 10:17f and 11:19, 24–26 definitely imply that He looked upon devil possession as a fact.[89]

It is clear from Arndt's argument that he accepted the reality of both the person of Satan and the phenomenon of demonic possession as biblical truths that continue into the modern world. However, Arndt anticipates that his readers will still question why there were so many cases of demonic possession during Jesus' time. Arndt answers:

> The only reply we can give is that Satan saw a Stronger Man than he had come to deprive him of his power, and he was now making a desperate effort to keep his dominions.[90]

---

[88] William F. Arndt, *Luke* (St. Louis: Concordia, 1984), 146.

[89] Arndt, *Luke*, 146.

[90] Arndt, *Luke*, 147.

Arndt's answer may also illuminate why there continues to be a
sizeable number of possessions in parts of the world where
Christianity is now making considerable strides among the peoples.
However, we might also do well to take his remarks as a warning to
our current situation and the increase of spiritualism found in our
times.

JEFFREY A. GIBBS

Gibbs is a professor of exegetical studies at Concordia Seminary,
St. Louis. Gibbs appreciates that many of his readers might find
difficulty with the possibility of exorcism in the present-day;
therefore he writes:

> What are we to think of demon possession in the world
> today? We cannot reject the possibility that some today may
> be possessed in the same way as the demoniacs were in 8:28–
> 29. Scripture does not promise that during this time before
> Christ returns, Satan and his angels have been bound so as
> never to enter and possess a human being, as these two men
> in the region of Gadarenes had experienced. However, two
> qualifications may be offered.[91]

Gibbs agrees that the problem of demoniacal possession remains
a concern in pastoral care. He is correct; Scripture does not promise
that Satan and his demon are incapable of possessing and harassing
people even now. However, there may be some difficulty with one of
the two qualifications that he offers. Gibbs continues:

> First, Scripture itself paints a suggestive picture. While the
> reality of the evil spirits is apparent throughout the OT and
> NT, accounts of demon possession are concentrated primarily
> in the Synoptic Gospels. There are precious few accounts of
> what we would call demon possession in the OT. Most of the
> OT, in fact, lacks any emphasis on direct demonic activity. In
> remarkable contrast, there is a dramatic emphasis on demon
> possession in the Synoptic Gospels, where the dominant
> theme of Jesus' message and ministry is the present reality
> and future promise of *the reign of God*. One might cautiously
> suggest that the great adversary and accuser threw his forces

---

[91] Gibbs, *Matthew 1:1–11:1*, 452.

into the fray in unprecedented fashion during the time when the Son of God was bringing God's royal reign near and driving back the old evil foe.[92]

The Scriptures affirm that in Christ's earthly ministry and continuing throughout the NT era, Satan is bound to an extent (Mt 12:22–29; Rev 20:2) so that he cannot prevent the Gospel from being proclaimed (Mt 24:14; 2Tim 2:24–26). Toward the end of this age Satan will be let loose for a short time (Rev 20:3). Moreover, the Scriptures picture Satan as being thrown out of heaven and defeated by the earthly ministry of Jesus, culminating in his death and resurrection (Lk 10:18; Jn 12:31; Col 2:15; Rev 12:5–10). As the Gospel is proclaimed throughout the world, Jesus continues to drive back Satan and his forces. Therefore, it should not surprise us if demonic possession is much rarer in our world and in our experience than it seems to have been in Palestine during Jesus' ministry. Jesus' numerous encounters with the demoniacs in the Synoptic Gospels testify that the time of his earthly ministry was unique in all the history of the creation. Ever since Jesus achieved the decisive victory at the cross and empty tomb, Satan and his hordes have been in retreat.[93]

Nevertheless, Scripture does not declare that such things as oppression and even possession by demons are impossible or unknown during this present time, perhaps especially among peoples and in lands where the Gospel has not yet been proclaimed widely or at all. Yet the church now lives in the confidence of Christ's first manifestation of the reign of heaven and in hopeful watching for his final and complete bringing of that reign at his second coming.[94]

Thus far, Gibbs' conclusions are in agreement with the arguments presented in this book. However, in his second suggestion there may be some discontinuity with the works of the previously noted theologians. The discontinuity is not with his exegesis, but with his conclusions. Gibbs writes:

---

[92] Gibbs, *Matthew 1:1–11:1*, 452.

[93] Gibbs, *Matthew 1:1–11:1*, 453.

[94] Gibbs, *Matthew 1:1–11:1*, 453.

A second suggestion, therefore, may be in order. What is clear from other parts of the NT is that all baptized believers in Christ have received the Spirit of God and are God's treasured possessions, with Christ living within (Rom 8:12–17; 1Cor 12:3; Gal 2:20; 4:4–7; Col 1:27; 1Jn 4:4). Therefore, no Christian could ever be indwelt or possessed by demons, or require exorcism as we see especially in the Synoptic Gospels, including Mt 8:28–32. God's children will surely be subject to the temptations and attacks of Satan. However, we do not need to fear demonic possession. For we are the followers of Jesus, who lives within us, and whose authority is incomparably greater than any demonic force (1Jn 4:4). In these latter days before the triune God ushers in our full salvation in the new heavens and the new earth (Revelation 21–22), the Son of God has given us the Holy Spirit in Baptism as his gift and down payment to vouchsafe our inheritance.[95]

Many Lutheran theologians in practice have given testimony to the reality of Christians becoming possessed, something which Gibbs seems to find problematic. The problem may be one of definitions. Who is a Christian? Does Baptism alone protect us against demoniacal possession? To this, the earlier Lutherans have said no. Christians are those who have been given the gift of faith and who gather around the means of grace. Yet, not all who gather at the altar of the Lord are members of the faith. Some gather for reasons other than the reception of Christ's gifts and the praise of thanksgiving. Such people appear to be Christians in their life manners, but internally remain amongst the unbelievers; these may be those who are open to demoniacal possession even though they are amongst the baptized. However, just like it is impossible to know the faith of anyone, it is likewise impossible to answer without a doubt if true Christians can be possessed. Walther and the early reformers thought that if such possession were to occur, it was allowed by the hand of God who was working for His own glory.[96]

---

[95] Gibbs, *Matthew 1:1–11:1*, 453.

[96] John 9:1–3.

FINAL THOUGHTS

This section has demonstrated that historic Lutheranism affirmed the reality of Satan, demons and diabolical possession. While at times modernism and rationalism have lessened this truth, it nevertheless has remained a confessional Lutheran teaching. From the formation of The Lutheran Church—Missouri Synod, both Walther and Pieper have continued to warn those who have dismissed the actions of Satan and diabolical possession as superstitions. Pastoral theologians, such as Fritz, Eyer, Thielicke, Montgomery, and Koch, have joined them in affirming the reality of present-day cases of diabolical possession. Modern exegetical theologians, who include Lenski, Arndt, and Gibbs, continue to bring warning of overlooking the demonic through their biblical commentaries. Even today, the warning must go out: Satan is active, and diabolical possession remains a pastoral problem that the Church must answer in the life of its people.

CHAPTER TEN

VISIT THIS HOUSE, O LORD

CONTEMPORARY CHURCHLY RESOURCES

Visit this house, O Lord. Drive far from it the evil one and let Your holy angel descend to dwell here.

—Lutheran Worship Agenda

Concordia Publishing House has continued to offer wonderful resources for use in both the church and home. This chapter will focus on resources that have been provided to pastors over recent years and review how demoniacal possession and protection from Satan has been handled. As with any resource produced by cultured institutions, we will find some to be exquisite while some may be lacking. We begin our chapter with the *The Lutheran Agenda* of 1966 and progress to the most recent of resources available to the church.

THE LUTHERAN AGENDA OF 1966

The Lutheran Agenda was published in 1966 for use in The Lutheran Church—Missouri Synod. It contains three Baptismal rites: one for the Baptism of infants with sponsors, one without sponsors and one for adults. All three rites include the Lord's Prayer and the renunciation of Satan. However, like other resources of its time, the Agenda contains no exorcism rites.[1] The rite provided for the

---

[1] Hans Naegeil Osjord notices that Baptism and exorcism have always been connected in Roman Catholicism. However, he notes that the Lutheran Church moved away from the connection between Baptism and exorcism in the 18th century. See Hans Naegeil Osjord, *Possession & Exorcism*, 59.

dedication of a dwelling lacks exorcistic language also. The opening prayer skimpily asks for God's presence to remain upon the dwelling:

> O Lord, almighty and eternal God, who hast permitted thy servants to erect this house, we entreat Thee to enter and abide therein, that the salvation of Thy kingdom may come to all that inhabit it, to that end that Thy name may be hallowed and all glory and worship be given unto Thee from this time forth and even forevermore. Amen.[2]

The closing prayer uses stronger language, but still refrains from using exorcistic language:

> Bless, O Lord, this house and what belongs hereto. Bless its inhabitants with true faith and a godly life, with zeal and faithfulness in Thy service. Bless them with health and strength in body and soul. Let Thy holy angels encamp around this house both day and night. Defend it against all danger, against fire and other calamities. Protect it with Thy mighty hand, and let all that dwell therein live in peace and happiness all the days of their lives. Unto Thee, the Father, the Son, and the Holy Ghost, be praise and glory forevermore. Amen.[3]

While the rite asks for the protection of holy angels, it purposely avoids any connotation of protecting from a "personal evil," like Satan or his demons. The only mention or request for protection from evil comes in the Lord's Prayer, which the rite suggests, "may be used" with the Benediction to close the rite. Yet, not all is lost. A new agenda for use in the church brings many benefits and provide some exceedingly helpful material to pastors. We now move on to the Lutheran Worship Agenda of 1984.

LUTHERAN WORSHIP AGENDA OF 1984

The *Lutheran Worship Agenda* was published in 1984 for use in The Lutheran Church—Missouri Synod. This Agenda is an improvement over its predecessor (*The Lutheran Agenda*). It contains two baptismal rites, one titled "Holy Baptism," and the other titled

---

[2] *The Lutheran Agenda* (St. Louis: Concordia, 1966), 185.

[3] *The Lutheran Agenda*, 186.

"Holy Baptism Short Form." The first rite, which is the longer of the two, continues in much the same manner as *The Lutheran Agenda*. Like its predecessor, The *Lutheran Worship Agenda* does not retain the exorcisms of Luther and the early Lutheran Church. Only the renunciation of Satan and the Lord's Prayer remain. No exorcism exists in the shorter rite. However, the newer Agenda makes a significant change to the section titled "The Dedication of a Dwelling" and "The Dedication of a Parsonage." This time an exorcistic command demands Satan to depart. Both of these documents contain similar language. Therefore, we will limit the discussion to the exorcism found in "The Dedication of a Dwelling":

> Visit this house, O Lord. Drive far from it the evil one and let your holy angel descend to dwell here. Preserve the people of this house that they may dwell in safety all the days of their lives and at the end enter your heavenly home; through Jesus Christ, your Son our Lord, who lives and reigns with you and the Holy Spirit, one God, now and forever.[4]

The exorcistic language used here is specific. The prayer asks the Lord to drive (exorcise) the "evil one" from the home. I have suggested this section of the Agenda to many pastors who have sought me out for assistance. While the next publication examined in this book provides tremendous improvements to all of the previous sources, we will find that when it comes to the section of dedication, the *Lutheran Worship Agenda* is still superior in its exorcistic language for use in pastoral visits to the home.

LUTHERAN SERVICE BOOK AGENDA OF 2006

> *Therefore, depart, you unclean spirit and make room for the Holy Spirit in the name of the Father and the Son and the Holy Spirit.*
>
> *—Lutheran Service Book*

The *Lutheran Service Book Agenda* was published in 2006 for use in The Lutheran Church—Missouri Synod. It contains three baptismal rites: "Holy Baptism," "Holy Baptism—Alternate Form Based on

---

[4] *Lutheran Worship Agenda* (St. Louis: Concordia, 1984), 339.

Luther's Baptismal Rite," and "Holy Baptism—In Case of Emergency."

The first of the baptismal rites attempts to bring the rite closer to Luther's of 1526. However, it excludes the exorcisms found in Luther's rite. This is the rite which is included in the official hymnal of the synod (*Lutheran Service Book*). Regretfully, the hymnal excludes the fuller rite making its assimilation into congregational setting difficult. This rite may cause confusion in the congregational setting because it differs from the printed version in the hymnal. The alternate rite states:

> Therefore, depart, you unclean spirit, and make room for the Holy Spirit in the name of the Father and the Son and the Holy Spirit.[5]

This addition accepts the reality of demoniacal possession. It brings continuity with the Lutheran Confessions, which accept the activity of the devil in the lives of both the faithful and unfaithful. Moreover, it specifically refers to the presiding statement of the rite, which reminds all the participants that without Christ, all are and remain in the hands of Satan whether physically possessed or not.

The final rite found in the Agenda is the shortened form for emergency Baptism. No renunciation of Satan or exorcism is included. This is understandable in emergency circumstances and a reminder that Baptism derives its power through the Word added to the water and not to the additional rites.

VISITATION: RESOURCES FOR THE CARE OF SOULS

One of the most useful resources provide for use in the church today comes in the form of Concordia Publishing House's recently released *Visitation* of 2008. This resource contains prayers and liturgical rites specifically directed to pastoral visitation. This book has been included in this section because of its emphasis on spiritual oppression and protection from the devil. It has four sections that deal specifically with this issue. The first section, titled "Spiritual Oppression" is an encouragement to those harassed by the devil. It directs believers to their Baptisms and reminds them that they are members of the Kingdom of God. The section states:

---

[5] *Lutheran Service Book Agenda* (St. Louis: Concordia, 2006), 13.

The devil is subtle. His portrayal in horror movies, that of horns and a spiked tail, is not true. Like a snake, the devil slithers his way into your life, takes you over, has you rationalizing your sins, and even worse, believing there is no spiritual battle to be fought.

The devil is real; evil is everywhere; demons are wrapped around you, slowly squeezing you to death. It is hopeless if you depend on yourself. You cannot fight the devil alone. You need Christ to fight for you . . . Jesus cloaks you with His victory.[6]

The section titled "Nature of Spiritual Warfare" assures the reader that the battle is won in Jesus. It provides a short liturgical rite for help when faced with spiritual warfare. It provides Psalm 3 for recitation and a short introduction speaking to the reality of spiritual warfare:

The presence of evil is real, and we are protected from the devil only through the power that comes from the name of Jesus. When confronted by the darkness of the devil, we will be protected by the living voice of Jesus in His Word, the strong name of the Trinity into which we are baptized, the confession of the Apostles' Creed, and the Lord's Prayer.[7]

This modern resource acknowledges the reality of spiritual warfare and the importance of the devotional use of Jesus' name in any struggle with the devil. It directs the reader to Psalm 53 and Luke 11:14–23. The liturgy continues with prayers, Psalms, and Scripture readings (Psalm 21, Luke 10:17–20, Ephesians 6:10–20, and Revelation 12:7–12.) Finally, it provides a concluding prayer which contains exorcistic language:

Jesus Christ, the very Word of God, who gave to Your holy apostles the power to trample underfoot serpents and scorpions, who is pleased to grant them the authority to say, "Depart, you devils!" and by whose might Satan was made to fall from heaven like lighting, I humbly call upon Your name

---

[6] Arthur A. Just Jr. and Scot A. Kinnaman, eds., *Visitation* (St. Louis: Concordia, 2008), 54.

[7] Just and Kinnaman, *Visitation*, 168.

in fear and trembling, asking You to grant this, Your servant, pardon for all sin, steadfast faith, and the power—supported by your mighty arm—to confront with confidence and resolution the cruel demon; through the same Jesus Christ, our Lord, who is coming to judge both the living and the dead.[8]

The liturgy then ends with an appropriate hymn.

While all the other resources described in this chapter were specifically provided for pastoral use, this last book, *Visitation*, is inexpensive and just as accessible to any Christian as the hymnals with which they are so familiar. A better liturgical resource is not available than *Visitation* for those seeking help with spiritual warfare.

---

[8] Just and Kinnaman, *Visitation*, 170.

CHAPTER ELEVEN

CONCLUSIONS AND FINAL THOUGHTS

CONCLUSIONS

This book has explored the experiences of those found within the *Fifohazana* movement of the Malagasy Lutheran Church. As we have learned, the Malagasy Lutheran Church has seen considerable growth in its membership over the past decade. However, up to this time little has been understood concerning what is actually occurring in that church. Some recent scholarship has focused upon its exorcism practices, but no research has gained access into the actual experiences of the converts, that is, through the experiences of those who have approached the church from the traditional religions. My hope for this book was to provide an insider's perspective into "lived experiences" of those who have experienced a conversion event leading them to Christianity, specifically, Malagasy Lutheran Christianity.

Through personal interviews this book opens to western eyes the life of the Spirit of our Malagasy brothers and sisters in Christ. The people we have encountered have told their own stories. While the research questions served as a guide, the constraints were more upon the interviewers than the respondents. The people were simply asked to "tell their story" within the context of their lives.

This book represents the lives of sixty-four recent converts to the Malagasy Lutheran Church. The seminary students of the SALT Seminary in Madagascar under the direction of Rev. Dr. Joseph Randrianasolo provided access to a group of individuals that would have taken years of research without their assistance. The Church will continually be blessed through their service and assistance in bringing these biblical truths to many who have forgotten these things or have tossed them away in search of greater knowledge. Dr. Randrianasolo must be commended for taking weeks out of his busy schedule to both translate the research questions in Malagasy and then back into English for the purpose of this book.

The findings of this book begin to unpack the inner workings of the traditional Malagasy mind by expressing the experiences of those who have undergone a conversion into the Christian Faith. What they demonstrate is a spiritual understanding remarkably close to the biblical worldview of early Christianity. This pre-modern worldview accepts the existence of a host of spiritual entities and openness to miracles.

The majority of those interviewed described either a spiritual struggle with the demonic or full body possessions at some time during their lives. The majority of respondents described the events surrounding their conversion in terms of their own exorcisms. The overwhelming response expressed by the converts was an experience of peace and freedom, which they had never felt before. Repeatedly the respondents expressed the word "release" as an explanation of their conversion. Moreover, the research also demonstrates the access points through which converts are drawn into the Church. The majority described their longing for peace and their recognition of the ability of the *mpiandry* to provide an answer to their quest. However, a strong evangelical character is also demonstrated within the Malagasy Lutheran Church, which travels into the remote countryside and preaches the Gospel where people live and work. The majority of the conversions recorded took place outside of the church building.

Other considerations uncovered are the strong catechesis model used by the church and the communal nature of its members. The Malagasy Lutheran Church has an advanced system of catechesis, which is directed at the lived experience of the people. This system incorporates intense study of the Holy Scriptures and Luther's Small Catechism with a practical aspect that deals directly with the experiences described in this research. Moreover, the majority of the converts spoke in Lutheran terms of Word and Sacrament, specifically pointing to their Baptisms and their inclusion with the Lord's Supper as means of continual growth and preservation in the faith.

THE SIGNIFICANCE OF THIS BOOK

This book is helpful to Christian churches because it demonstrates the effectiveness of Christianity within an animistic context. In view of this research, The Lutheran Church in Madagascar is the only Malagasy Christian denomination dealing directly with the spiritual worldview of the people. Other denominations have either accepted the traditional practices, creating acceptable syncretism which becomes Christian animism, or ignored the traditional worldview, causing a hidden syncretism or folk religion to exist alongside the western leading worldview of the previous colonial powers. By dealing directly with the people within their context, the Malagasy Lutherans have been able to reduce the problem of syncretism within their denomination.

As the western worldview continues to shift toward animism and the philosophy surrounding post-modernity, western views of rationalism appear to be on the decline and a new acceptance of the spiritualism seems to be the way of the future. If this is true, the Malagasy Lutheran Church's methods of contextualized catechesis and exorcism may lead the way to reach the lost within the western world.

THE CONTRIBUTIONS OF THIS BOOK

This book provides an insight into a phenomenon found within the Malagasy Lutheran Church that is just beginning to be uncovered by western researchers. It adds to the recent scholarship begun by Hans Austnaberg and Cynthia Holder-Rich by providing an even greater glimpse into the use of exorcism by telling the stories of those who have undergone this phenomenon and are now active leaders in the Confessional Movement of the Malagasy Lutheran Church.

EMERGING QUESTIONS DESERVING FUTURE RESEARCH

MARTIN LUTHER'S SMALL CATECHISM AND CONTEXTUALIZATION

This research has uncovered a key tool in the arsenal of the Malagasy Lutheran Church, namely, its contextualized use and teaching of Luther's Small Catechism. Additional research into the catechesis models employed by the Malagasy Lutherans and how these models address the questions of the recently converted would be extremely helpful especially to those converts who have entered the Church through exorcisms and spiritual battles.

EXORCISM AND HEALING IN WESTERN CONGREGATIONAL LIFE

Another emerging question relates to the possibility of incorporating the rite of exorcism into modern-day western congregation life. Could the Malagasy model be incorporated into western Christianity, specifically within Lutheran denominations? What would it look like and what would be necessary for its enculturation? One possibility for future inquiry could be the Malagasy *toby* system and possible implantations of such a system through the concept of mercy work currently found within the LCMS World Relief and Human Care.

EFFECTS OF THE *MPIANDRY* MOVEMENT UPON SEMINARY EDUCATION

During the research, it was discovered that a significant number of Lutheran pastors had described their call into the Holy Ministry through their experience with the *mpiandry* movement of the *Fifohazana*. Although I have written a short journal article referring to this phenomenon, additional research would be helpful.[1]

THE "DARK FIGURE"—COMMON PHENOMENON?

The research found a large number of respondents who reported the appearance of a "dark figure" who appeared to them during their possession/oppression experience. Other research has described similar events in unrelated cultures.[2] Is this a common phenomenon found in humanity?

---

[1] Robert H. Bennett, "The Missiological Impact of the Mpiandry Movement upon Theological Education in the Malagasy Lutheran Church," *Missio Apostolica* 16, no. 2, 32nd ser. (November 2008): 139.

[2] Leslie Shepard, Lewis Spence, and Nandor Fodor, eds., *Encyclopedia of Occultism & Parapsychology*, vol. 2 (Detroit, MI: Gale Research, 1984), s.v. "Haunting."

APPENDIX ONE

TABLES AND CROSS TABULATIONS

Table 1. Previous Religious Background

	Frequency	Valid Percent
Traditional Religion	38	59.4
Traditional Religion / Roman Catholic	11	17.2
Traditional Religion / Islam	8	12.5
Islam	1	1.6
Roman Catholic	1	1.6
Lutheran	1	1.6
Other	2	3.1
Reformed	1	1.6
Traditional Religion / Lutheran	1	1.6
Total	64	100.0

Table 2. Previous Spiritual Allegiance

	Frequency	Valid Percent	Cumulative Percent
Razana	11	17.2	17.2
Spirits	4	6.2	23.4
Ombiasy	39	60.9	84.4
Other	9	14.1	98.4
No Response	1	1.6	100.0
Total	64	100.0	

Table 3. Perceived Benefits from Spiritual Affiliation

	Frequency	Valid Percent	Cumulative Percent
Blessings	42	65.6	65.6
Knowledge	8	12.5	78.1
Power	5	7.8	85.9
Other	9	14.1	100.0
Total	64	100.0	

Table 4. Perceived To Receive Healing by Razana

	Frequency	Valid Percent	Cumulative Percent
Yes	23	35.9	35.9
No	41	64.1	100.0
Total	64	100.0	

Table 5. Respondents Self-Identified as Possessed

	Frequency	Valid Percent	Cumulative Percent
Yes	35	54.7	54.7
No	27	42.2	96.9
No Response	2	3.1	100.0
Total	64	100.0	

Table 6. Pre-converted State of Health

	Frequency	Valid Percent	Cumulative Percent
Had illness	34	53.1	53.1
No illness	6	9.4	62.5
Someone close had illness	13	20.3	82.8
In Fear	7	10.9	93.8
Other	3	4.7	98.4
No Response	1	1.6	100.0
Total	64	100.0	

Table 7. Cross Tabulation: Has Been Possessed vs. Physical/Mental/Spiritual Experience

		Physical/Mental/Spiritual Experience						
		Had illness	No illness	Someone close had an illness	In Fear	Other	No Response	Total
Has Been Possessed	Yes	23	3	5	4	0	0	35
	No	9	3	8	3	3	1	27
	No Response	2	0	0	0	0	0	2
	Total	34	6	13	7	3	1	64

Table 8. Family Connection to the Malagasy Lutheran Church

	Frequency	Valid Percent	Cumulative Percent
Yes	36	56.2	56.2
No	27	42.2	98.4
No Response	1	1.6	100.0
Total	64	100.0	

Table 9. Previous Religious Allegiance and Family Connection to the Malagasy Lutheran Church

	Family / Friends in FLM.			
	Yes	No	No Response	Total
Traditional Religion	18	19	1	38

Table 10. Reasons for Approaching the Malagasy Lutheran Church

	Frequency	Valid Percent	Cumulative Percent
Saw a mystical vision	2	3.1	3.1
Healed by Exorcism	11	17.2	20.3
Family / Friend healed by Exorcism	4	6.2	26.6
By request from family / friend	4	6.2	32.8
Evangelized by Christian	24	37.5	70.3
Sought freedom from Spirits / Ancestors (Razana)	12	18.8	89.1
Other	6	9.4	98.4
No Response	1	1.6	100.0
Total	64	100.0	

Table 11. Conversion Location

	Frequency	Valid Percent	Cumulative Percent
Home	10	15.6	15.6
Toby	16	25.0	40.6
Church	23	35.9	76.6
Unspecified	12	18.8	95.3
No Response	3	4.7	100.0
Total	64	100.0	

Table 12. Cross tabulation: Previous Possession
vs. Location of Conversion

Has Been Possessed: Location of Conversion Event Cross Tabulation							
		Location of Conversion Event					
		Home	Toby	Church	Unspecified	No Response	Total
Has Been Possessed	Yes	6	13	7	8	1	35
	No	3	3	15	4	2	27
	No Response	0	1	1	0	0	2
	Total	9	17	23	12	3	64

Table 13. Pre-conversion Phenomenon

	Frequency	Valid Percent	Cumulative Percent
Doubt in Traditional Religion	9	14.1	14.1
Mystical Vision of Jesus	4	6.2	20.3
Sorrow Over Sin & Internal Strife	14	21.9	42.2
Struggled with the Spirits	26	40.6	82.8
Other	10	15.6	98.4
No Response	1	1.6	100.0
Total	64	100.0	

Table 14. Conversion Phenomenon

	Frequency	Valid Percent	Cumulative Percent
Experienced Repentance from previous state	21	33.3	33.3
Mystical Vision of Jesus	2	3.2	36.5
Peace, Freedom, Trust	20	31.7	68.3
Mystical Vision of Evil Spirits	4	6.3	74.6
Other	13	20.6	95.2
No Response	3	4.8	100.0
Total	63	100.0	

Table 15. Cross Tabulation: Has Been Possessed vs. Conversion Experience

Previously Possessed	Experienced Repentance for previous state	Mystical Vision of Jesus	Peace, Freedom, Trust	Mystical Vision of Evil Spirits	Other	No Response	Total
Yes	7	1	15	3	7	2	35
No	13	1	5	1	5	1	26
No Response	1	0	0	0	1	0	2
Total	21	2	20	4	13	3	63

Table 16. Post-Conversion Experience

	Frequency	Valid Percent	Cumulative Percent
Experienced Repentance	9	14.1	14.1
Mystical Vision of Jesus	2	3.1	17.2
Freedom, Peace, Trust	46	71.9	89.1
Other	3	4.7	93.8
No Response	4	6.2	100.0
Total	64	100.0	

Table 17. Post-Conversion Extended Change

	Frequency	Valid Percent	Cumulative Percent
Became Mpiandry	8	12.7	12.7
Became Pastor	3	4.8	17.5
Became other Church Leader	1	1.6	19.0
Experience Peace and Forgiveness	22	34.9	54.0
Experience Freedom from Spiritual Oppression	18	28.6	82.5
Unidentified + Change	8	12.7	95.2
No response	3	4.8	100.0
Total	63	100.0	

Table 18. Current Religious Allegiance

	Frequency	Valid Percent	Cumulative Percent
Jesus	38	59.4	59.4
Pastor	7	10.9	70.3
Church	10	15.6	85.9
Other	4	6.2	92.2
No Response	5	7.8	100.0
Total	64	100.0	

Table 19. Cross Tabulation: Pre-conversion Allegiance vs. Post-conversion Religious Allegiance

		Current Religious Allegiance					
		Jesus	Pastor	Church	Other	No Response	Total
Previous Religious Allegiance	Razana	6	2	1	1	1	11
	Spirits	3	1	0	0	0	4
	Ombiasy	24	4	7	2	2	39
	Other	4	0	2	1	2	9
	No Response	1	0	0	0	0	1
	Total	38	7	10	4	5	64

Table 20. Post-Conversion Syncretism

Syncretism	Frequency	Valid Percent	Cumulative Percent
No	56	87.5	87.5
No Response	8	12.5	100.0
Total	64	100.0	

Table 21. Churchly Provisions

	Frequency	Valid Percent	Cumulative Percent
Word & Sacrament	33	51.6	51.6
Prayer	2	3.1	54.7
Faith	9	14.1	68.8
Other	12	18.8	87.5
No Response	8	12.5	100.0
Total	64	100.0	

APPENDIX TWO

FIELD MATERIAL

The interviews recorded represent respondents from ten of the twenty-two regions of Madagascar (see bold print below). A numerical code has been assigned to each region. This code will help to establish a standardized method of representing the field interviews presented within this research. Therefore, the interviews will be abbreviated in the following formula, S#GR

S = student conducted interview

\# = random number assigned to interview

G = gender of respondent

R = number of assigned region represented by interview

Therefore, the S1M11 would represent Student interview 1, Male, region 11

REGIONS OF MADAGASCAR

1. Diana
2. Sofia
3. **Boeny**
4. **Melaky**
5. **Menabe**
6. **Atsimo-Andrefana**
7. Androy
8. Sava
9. **Analanjirofo**
10. **Atsinanana**
11. **Vatovaxy Fitovinany**

12. Atsimi Atsinanana
13. Betsiboka
14. Analamanga
15. Bongolava
16. **Alaotra Mangoro**
17. Itasy
18. Vakinankaratra
19. Amoron 'I Mania
20. **Matsatra Ambony**
21. **Ihorombe**
22. Anosy

LIST OF FIELD INTERVIEWS

Represented below are the interviews included within the research. If the region is unknown, '00' is inserted for the region section.

S01M11	S25F05	S49F11
S02M03	S26F05	S50F09
S03M04	S27F10	S51F21
S04M04	S28M05	S52F16
S05M05	S29M05	S53F11
S06M05	S30M10	S54M11
S07M00	S31M21	S55F16
S08M11	S32F06	S56M10
S09M11	S34F04	S57M06
S10M04	S35M06	S58M10
S11M11	S36F05	S59M06
S12F05	S36F05	S60M10
S13F05	S37M00	S61M06
S14F11	S38F04	S62M10
S15M11	S39F20	S63M21
S16M11	S40F11	S64F21
S17M11	S41M06	S65M04
S18M04	S42M10	S66M10
S19M21	S43M11	S67F16
S20M10	S44M11	S68M20
S21M11	S45F06	S69F20
S22F20	S46F06	S70M10
S23M04	S47F10	S72M21
S24F05	S48F11	S73F15

INTERVIEW IN MALAGASY LANGUAGE

FANADIHADIANA FIKAROHANA

FIVAVAHANA TEO *ALOHA* (Ny nahazo anao sy ny fivavahana narahinao talohan'ny ny naha-Loterana)

1. Lazalazao ny fivavahana narahinao teo aloha
2. Iza no nantoninao hanampy anao amin'ny fiainanao? (ombiasy, razana, olon-tsotra, pretra, kristiana, jesosy, Pastora . . .). Inona no fanampiana azonao?
3. Ahoana ny fifandraisanao amin'ny razana? (famadihana, tsodrano, fitahiana, ozona . . .)
4. Efa nahazo fitahiana na fanasitranana avy amin'ny razana ve ianao? Tantarao.
5. Efa nipetrahan'ny razana ve ianao? (tromba, bilo, doany, kasoa, ambalavelo, sisiky, maso be tsy mahita . . .)

NY NAHAZO ANAO? (ny nahatonga anao ho Loterana)

1. Inona no nahazo anao? (aretina, tsy fahombiazana . . .)
2. Moa manana fianakaviana na namama ao amin'ny Fiangonana Loterana Malagasy ianao?
3. Oviana no niheveranao ho tonga Loterana? Tantarao.
4. Oviana no nibebahanao ka nahatapa-kevitra anao ho Loterana? Tantarao. Taiza no nitrangan'izany? (Fiangonana, trano, arabe, toby . . .)

NY FITRANGAN'NY *FIBEBAHANA* (ny nitranga, ny adimpanahy, ny aretina sy ny nahazoanao nandritra ny fibebahanao.)

1. Inona no tsapanao talohan'ny nibebahanao? (inona no hitanao, fofona renao, fahatsapana amin;ny fikasihana . . .)
2. Tamin'ny nibebahanao, inona no tsapanao?

3. Inona notsapanao nanaraka ny nibebahanao?

NY NITRANGA TAORIAN'NY FIBEBAHANA (Ny fitaizana sy ny fitahiana ary ny fahasoavana azonao *tamin'ny* nahaLoterana anao)

1. Misy fiovana ve tamin'ny fiainanao amin'izao fotoana izao hatramin'ny nandaozanao ny fivavahana tamin'ny razana teo aloha? (na koa fivavahana hafa)

2. Iza no antoninao hanampy anao amin'ny fiainanao (ombiasy, razana, olon-tsotra, pretra, kristiana, Jesosy, Pastora ...). Inona no fanampiana azonao? Mbola manphy mitady azy ireo ve ianao?

3. Ahoana ny fifaneraseranano tamin'ny maty (razana) teo aloha?

4. Inona no nataon'ny Fiangonana taminao mba handresenao ny olana misy eo aminao ka tsy hanatonanao intsony ny fanahin'ny maty?

BIBLIOGRAPHY

Allen, Philip M. *Historical Dictionary of Madagascar*. Lanham: Scarecrow Press, 2005.

Allison, Dale, and W. D. Davies. *A Critical and Exegetical Commentary on the Gospel According to Saint Matthew*, vol. 2 of 4. Edinburgh: T&T Clark, 1998.

Anderson, Allan H. "Exorcism and Conversion to African Pentecostalism." *Exchange* 35, no. 1 (2006): 116–33.

Anderson, Gerald H., ed. *Biographical Dictionary of Christian Missions*. Grand Rapids: Eerdmans, 1999.

Anderson, Neil T. *The Bondage Breaker: Overcoming Negative Thoughts, Irrational Feelings and Habitual Sins*. New York: Harvest House Publishers, 2006.

Arndt, William F. *Luke*. St. Louis: Concordia, 1984.

Ashqar, 'Umar Sulaymān. *World of the Jinn & Devils in the Light of the Qur'an and Sunnah*. Riyadh: International Islamic Publishing House, 2003.

Austnaberg, Hans. *Shepherds and Demons: A Study of Exorcism As Practiced and Understood by Shepherds in the Malagasy Lutheran Church*. Bible and Theology in Africa. New York: Peter Lang, 2007.

Beck, James R., and Gordon R. Lewis. "Counseling and the Demonic: A Reaction to Page." *Journal of Psychology and Theology* 17, no. 2 (1989): 132–34.

Bediako, Kwame. *Christianity in Africa: The Renewal of a Non-Western Religion*. Edinburgh: Edinburgh University Press, Orbis Books, 1995.

Bennett, Robert H. "The Missiological Impact of the Mpiandry Movement upon Theological Education in the Malagasy Lutheran Church." *Missio Apostolica* 16, no. 2, 32nd ser. (November 2008): 139–47.

Bercot, David W., ed. *Dictionary of Early Christian Beliefs: A Reference Guide to More than 700 Topics Discussed by the Early Church Fathers*. Peabody: Hendrickson Publishers, 1998.

Best, Ernest. "Dead in Trespasses and Sins (Eph 2:1)." *Journal for the Study of the New Testament* 13 (1981): 9–25.

_____. "Ephesians: Two Types of Existence." *Interpretation* 47, no. 1 (1993): 39–51.

Bible Works. Computer software. Version 4.0. Norfolk: Bible Works, 2007.

Blamires, Harry. *The Christian Mind: How Should a Christian Think?* Grand Rapids: Regent College Publishing, 2005.

Bloch, Maurice. *From Blessing to Violence: History and Ideology in the Circumcision Ritual of the Merina of Madagascar*. Cambridge: Cambridge University Press, 1986.

_____. *Placing the Dead: Tombs, Ancestral Villages, and Kinship Organization in Madagascar*. Prospect Heights: Waveland Press, 1971.

Botokeky, Eléonore Nerine. "Le Fitampoha en Royaume de Menabe, in Les Souverains de Madagascar." Translated by Joseph Randrianasolo. In *L'Histoire Royale et se Résurgences Contemporaines*, edited by Françoise Raison-Jourde, 199–211. Paris: Karthala, 1983.

Bourguignon, Erika. *Possession*. San Francisco: Chandler & Sharp Publishers, 1976.

Bryant, M. Darrol, Lewis R. Rambo, and Charles E. Farbadian. "Converting: Stages of Religious Change." Edited by Christopher Lamb. In *Religious Conversion: Contemporary Practices and Controversies*, 23–34. London: Cassell, 1999.

Bull, Dennis L. "A Phenomenological Model of Therapeutic Exorcism For Dissociative Identity Disorder." *Journal of Psychology and Theology* 29, no. 2 (2001): 131–39.

_____. "Exorcism Revisited: Positive Outcomes With Dissociative Identity Disorder." *Journal of Psychology and Theology* 26, no. 2 (1998): 188–89.

Burgess, Andrew. *RA-HA-LA-HI-KO: My Brother in Madagascar*. Minneapolis: Augsburg, 1938.

_____. *Zanahary In Madagascar*. Minneapolis: Board of Foreign Missions, 1932.

Burnett, David. *Unearthly Powers: A Christian's Handbook on Primal and Folk Religions*. Nashville: Oliver Nelson, 1992.

Byrne, Brendan. *Costly Freedom: A Theological Reading of Mark's Gospel*. Collegeville: Liturgical Press, 2008.

Carus, Paul. *History of the Devil and the Idea of Evil*. New York: Gramercy Books, 1996.

"Catholic Encyclopedia: Madagascar." New Advent: Home. http://www.newadvent.org/cathen/09509e.htm (accessed November 06, 2009).

"C. F. W. Walther." Concordia Historical Institute: Department of Archives and History, LCMS. http://chi.lcms.org/presidents/pres_walther.htm (accessed July 05, 2010).

Chemnitz, Martin. *Examination of the Council of Trent.* Translated by Fred Kramer. Vol. 2. St. Louis: Concordia, 1986.

_____. *Loci Theologici*. Translated by Jacob A. O. Preus. St. Louis: Concordia, 1989.

The Christian Mission Among Rural Peoples. Vol. 3. Lebanon: Foreign missions Conference of North America, 1945.

Cole, Jennifer. *Forget Colonialism? Sacrifice and the Art of Memory in Madagascar*. Berkeley: University of California Press, 2001.

_____. "Sacrifice, Narratives and Experience in East Madagascar." *Journal of Religion in Africa* 27, no. 4 (1997): 401–25.

Commentary on the New Testament Use of the Old Testament. Grand Rapids: Baker Academic, 2007.

Corrie, John, ed. *Dictionary of Mission Theology Evangelical Foundations*. Grand Rapids: InterVarsity Press, 2007.

Creswell, John W. *Research Design: Qualitative, Quantitative, and Mixed Methods Approaches*. 2nd ed. Minneapolis: Sage Publications, Inc., 2002.

Cullmann, Oscar. *The Christology of the New Testament*. New York: Westminster John Knox Press, 1980.

Dickason, C. Fred. *Demon Possession and the Christian: A New Perspective*. New York: Crossway Books, 1989.

Domenichini-Ramiaramanana, Bakoly. "The Church and Malagasy Culture." *Exchange* 22, no. 1 (1993): 46–64.

Dronen, Toma S. "A Missionary Discourse on Conversion: Norwegian Missionaries in Adamawa, North Cameroon 1934–1960." *Mission Studies: Journal of the International Association for Mission Studies* 24, no. 1 (2007): 99–126.

Elert, Werner. *The Christian Ethos*. Translated by Carl J. Scindler. Philadelphia: Muhlenberg Press, 1957.

Emoff, Ron. *Recollecting from the Past: Musical Practice and Spirit Possession on the East Coast of Madagascar* (Music Culture). Middletown: Wesleyan, 2002.

Eyer, Richard C. *Pastoral Care Under the Cross: God in the Midst of Suffering*. St. Louis: Concordia, 1994.

Fabella, Virginia. *Dictionary of Third World Theologies*. New York: Orbis Books, 2003.

Ferdinando, Keith. *The Triumph of Christ in African Perspective* (Paternoster Theological Monographs). Grand Rapids: Paternoster, 1969.

Ferguson, Sinclair B., David F. Wright, and J. I. Packer. *New Dictionary of Theology*. Downers Grove: InterVarsity Press, 1988.

"Fiangonana Loterana Malagasy eto Paris - Recherche: mpiandry." Fiangonana Loterana Malagasy eto Paris - page d'accueil. http://www.flmparis.org/tags/mpiandry (accessed November 06, 2009).

Flavius, Josephus. *Works of Josephus: Complete and Unabridged*. Peabody: Hendrickson Publishers, 1987.

Fritz, John H. C. *Pastoral Theology*. St. Louis: Concordia, 2003.

Fuglestad, Finn. *Norwegian Missions in African History: Volume 2 Madagascar* (Norwegian University Press Publication). New York: Oxford University Press, USA, 1987.

Gaebelein, Frank E. *The Expositor's Bible Commentary: John and Acts*. Vol. 9. Grand Rapids: Zondervan, 1984.

Gennep, Arnold V. *The Rites of Passage*. Chicago: University of Chicago Press, 1960.

Gibbs, Jeffrey A. *Matthew 1:1–11:1*. Concordia Commentary. St. Louis: Concordia, 2006.

Gilbert, Pierre. "Further Reflections on Paul Hiebert's; The Flaw of the Excluded Middle." *Direction* 36, no. 2 (Fall 2007): 206–18.

Gombis, Timothy. "Ephesians 2 as a Narrative of Divine Warfare." *Journal for the Study of the New Testament* 4 (2004): 403–18.

González-Wippler, Migene. *Complete Book of Amulets & Talismans*. Woodbury: Llewellyn Publications, 2005.

Green, Michael. "Conversion." In *Evangelism in the Early Church*, 144–65. Grand Rapids: Eerdmans, 1985.

Grundmann, Christoffer H. "Inviting the Spirits To Fight The Spirits? Pneumatological Challenges for Missions in Healing and Exorcism." *International Review of Missions* 94, no. 372 (January 2005): 51–73.

Halverson, Alton C.O. *Madagascar: Footprint at the End of The World*. Minneapolis: Augsburg, 1973.

Harries, Jim. "The Magical Worldview in the African Church: What Is Going On?" *Missiology* 28, no. 4 (October 2000): 487–502.

Hiebert, Paul G. *Anthropological Insights for Missionaries*. Grand Rapids: Baker Book House, 1985.

_____. *Incarnational Ministry: Planting Churches in Band, Tribal, Peasant and Urban Societies*. Grand Rapids: Baker Books, 1995.

_____, R. Daniel Shaw, and Tite Tiénou. *Understanding Folk Religion: A Christian Response to Popular Beliefs and Practices*. Grand Rapids: Baker Academic, 2000.

_____. "Spiritual Warfare and Worldviews." *Direction* 29, no. 2 (2000): 114–24.

_____. "The Flaw of the Excluded Middle." *Missiology* 10, no. 1 (January 1982): 35–47.

Hill, Harriet. "Witchcraft and the Gospel: Insights from Africa." *Missiology: An International Review* 24, no. 3 (July 1996): 323–44.

Hio-Kee Ooi, Samuel. "A Study of Strategic Level Spiritual Warfare from a Chinese Perspective." *Asian Journal of Pentecostal Studies* 9, no. 1 (2006): 143–61.

Holder-Rich, Cynthia, ed. *The Fifohazana: Madagascar's Indigenous Christian Movement*. Amherst: Cambria press, 2008.

———. "Spirits and the Spirit: The Ministry of Madagascar's Healing Shepherds." *Religion and Theology* 13, no. 1 (2006): 54–71.

Hultgren, Arland J., and Steven A. Haggmark, eds. *The Earliest Christian Heretics readings from their Opponents*. Minneapolis: Fortress Press, 1996.

Hurtado, Larry W. *Lord Jesus Christ: Devotion to Jesus in Earliest Christianity*. Boston: Eerdmans, 2003.

Isichei, Elizabeth Allo. *History of Christianity in Africa from Antiquity to the Present*. Grand Rapids: Eerdmans, Africa World Press, 1995.

Jahn, Richard C. "The Doctrine of Angels." In *The Abiding Word: Doctrinal Essays for 1954–1955*, by Laetsch, 184–243. Vol. 3. St. Louis: Concordia, 2003.

Just, Arthur A., Jr. *Luke 1:1–9:50*. Concordia Commentary. St. Louis: Concordia, 1996.

———, and Scot A. Kinnaman, eds. *Visitation*. St. Louis: Concordia, 2008.

JWM home. http://www.jwm.christendom.co.uk/ (accessed December 30, 2009).

Keener, Craig S. *IVP Bible Background Commentary New Testament*. Downers Grove: InterVarsity Press, 1993.

Keller, Eva. *The Road to Clarity: Seventh-Day Adventism in Madagascar*. New York: Palgrave Macmillan, 2005.

Kittel, Gerhard, Geoffrey William Bromiley, and Gerhard Friedrich. *Theological Dictionary of the New Testament*. Vol. 1. Grand Rapids: Eerdmans, 1964

Klutz, Todd. *The Exorcism Stories in Luke-Acts: A Sociostylistic Reading* (Society for New Testament Studies Monograph Series). New York: Cambridge University Press, 2004.

Koch, Kurt E. *Between Christ and Satan*. Berghausen Bd.: Evangelization Publishers, 1961.

_____. *Christian Counseling and Occultism: A Complete Guidebook to Occult Oppression and Deliverance*. Minneapolis: Kregel Publications, 1972.

_____. *Demonology Past and Present: Identifying and Overcoming Demonic Strongholds*. Grand Rapids: Kregel Publications, 2000.

Kolb, Robert, and Timothy J. Wengert, eds. *The Book of Concord: The Confessions of the Evangelical Lutheran Church*. New York: Augsburg Fortress, 2001.

Kraft, Charles H. *Defeating Dark Angels: Breaking Demonic Oppression in the Believer's Life*. Ventura: Regal Books, 2004.

Lane, William L. *The Gospel According to Mark*. Grand Rapids: Eerdmans, 1974.

Lassiter, James E. "African Culture And Personality: Bad Social Science, Effective Social Activism, Or A Call To Reinvent Ethnology?" African Studies Quarterly. http://web.africa.ufl.edu/asq/v3/v3i3a1.htm (accessed June 24, 2010).

Lehmann, Arthur C., and James E. Myers. *Magic, Witchcraft, and Religion: An Anthropological Study of the Supernatural*. Mountain View: Mayfield, 1997.

Lenski, R. C. H. *The Interpretation of St. Mark's Gospel*. Columbus: Wartburg Press, 1946.

_____. *The Interpretation of St. Matthew's Gospel*. Columbus: Wartburg Press, 1943.

_____. *The Interpretation of John's Gospel*. Columbus: Wartburg Press, 1942.

_____. *The Interpretation of St. Luke's Gospel*. Columbus: Wartburg Press, 1946.

Lewis, Ioan M. *Estatic Religion: An Anthropological Study of Spirit Possession and Shamanism*. Harmondsworth: Penguin Books, 1971.

Logos Bible Software. Computer software. Version 4.0. Oak Harbor: Logos Research Systems, Inc., 2006.

Ludwig, Garth D. *Order Restored: A Biblical Interpretation of Health, Medicine, and Healing.* St. Louis: Concordia Academic Press, 1999.

Lueker, Erwin Louis. *Lutheran Cyclopedia: A Concise In-Home Reference for The Christian Family.* Electronic ed. St. Louis: Concordia, 1984.

Luther, Martin. *Luther's Works (Liturgy and Hymns AE 53).* Edited by Helmut T. Lehmann. Translated by Paul Zeller Strodach. 55 vols. New York: Augsburg Fortress Publishers, 1965.

The Lutheran Agenda. St. Louis: Concordia, 1966.

Lutheran Service Book Agenda. St Louis: Concordia, 2006.

Lutheran Worship Agenda. St. Louis: Concordia, 1984.

Malony, Newton H., and Samuel Southard. *Handbook of Religious Conversion.* Birmingham: Religious Education Press, 1992.

Matson, William A. *The Adversary, His Person, Power and Purpose: A Study in Satanology.* Grand Rapids: Kessinger Publishing, 2005.

McElroy, Colleen J. *Over the Lip of the World: Among the Storytellers of Madagascar* (Samuel & Althea Stroum Books). New York: University of Washington Press, 1999.

McLeod, Lyons. *Madagascar and Its People.* New York: Negro Universities Press, 1969.

Meigs, Thomas. "Pastoral Care Methods And Demonology In Selected Writings." *Pastoral Psychology and Christian Education* 5, no. 3 (Fall 1977): 234–46.

Mentzer, Balthasar. *Balthasar Mentzer's Handbook.* Translated by Walter Hamester. Decatur: St. Anselm Press, 1998.

Middleton, Karen. *Ancestors, Power and History in Madagascar* (Studies of Religion in Africa). New York: Brill Academic Publishers, 1999.

Milingo, Emmanuel. *World in Between Christian Healing and the Struggle for Spiritual Survival.* London: C. Hurst, Orbis Books, 1984.

Montgomery, John Warwick, ed. *Demon Possession: A Medical, Historical, Anthropological, and Theological Symposium: Papers*

Presented at the University of Notre Dame, January 8–11, 1975, Under the Auspices of the Christian Medical Society. Minneapolis: Bethany Fellowship, 1975.

_____. *Principalities and Powers: The World of the Occult.* Minneapolis: Pyramid Publications for Bethany Fellowship, 1975.

Moreau, A. Scott. *The World of Spirits: A Biblical Study in the African Context.* Nairobi: Evangel, 1990.

_____, ed. *Evangelical Dictionary of World Missions* (Baker Reference Library). Grand Rapids: Baker Academic, 2000.

Morris, Leon. *The Gospel According to John.* Grand Rapids: Eerdmans, 1995.

Mueller, John Theodore, and Franz Pieper. *Christian Dogmatics: A Handbook of Doctrinal Theology for Pastors, Teachers, and Laymen.* St. Louis: Concordia, 1934.

Mueller, Norbert H., and George Kraus, eds. *Pastoral Theology.* St. Louis: Concordia, 1990.

Nida, Eugene A., and William A. Smalley. *Introducing Animism.* New York: Friendship Press, 1959.

Nock, A. D. *Conversion: The Old and the New in Religion from Alexander the Great to Augustine of Hippo.* Oxford: Oxford University Press, 1933.

Nürnberger, Klaus. *Living Dead and the Living God: Christ and the Ancestors in a Changing Africa.* Pietermaritzburg, South Africa: Cluster Publications, C. B. Powell Bible Centre, 2007.

Oesterreich, Traugott Konstantin. *Possession: Demoniacal and Other.* Grand Rapids: Kessinger Publishing, 2003.

Ogbu, Kalu. "Preserving a Worldview: Pentecostalism in the African Maps of the Universe." *Pneuma* 24, no. 2 (Fall 2002): 110–37.

Okorocha, Cyril C. "Religious Conversion in Africa: its Missiological Implications." *Missions Studies* 9, no. 2 (1992): 161–81.

Olson, Ken. *Exorcism: Fact or Fiction.* Nashville: T. Nelson, 1992.

Onyinab, Opoku. "Contemporary "Witchdemonology" in Africa." *International Review of Mission* 95, no. 3701371 (October 2004): 330–45.

Ooi, Samuel Hio-Kee. "A Study of Strategic Level Spiritual Warfare From a Chinese Perspective." *Asian Journal of Pentecostal Studies* 9, no. 1 (2006): 143–61.

Osjord, Hans Naegeil. *Possession & Exorcism*. Oregon: New Frontiers Center, 1988.

Otis, George. *Last of the Giants*. Tarrytown: Chosen Books, 1991.

Page, Sydney H. T. "The Role of Exorcism in Clinical Practice and Pastoral Care." *Journal of Psychology and Theology* 17, no. 2 (1989): 121–31.

Pare, Philip. *God Made the Devil? A Ministry of Healing*. London: Darton, Longman, and Todd, 1985.

Patton, Michael Quinn. *Qualitative Research and Evaluation Methods*. Thousand Oaks: Sage Publications, 2002.

Penn-Lewis, Jessie, and Evan Roberts. *War on the Saints: A Text Book on the Work of Deceiving Spirits Among the Children of God, and a Way of Deliverance*. New York: Diggory Press, 2005.

Pieper, Francis. *Christian Dogmatics. (1950). Vol. 1–4*. Vol. 2. Saint Louis: Concordia, 1960.

Powlison, David A. *Power Encounters: Reclaiming Spiritual Warfare* (Hourglass Books). New York: Baker Books, 1995.

Preus, Herman. *The Doctrine of Man*. St. Louis: Concordia, 2006.

Price, Charles T. *Missionary to the Malagasy: The Madagascar Diary of the Rev. Charles T. Price, 1875–1877*. New York: P. Lang, 1989.

Ramambason, Laurent W. Missiology: *Its Subject-Matter and Method: A Study Of Mission-Doers In Madagascar* (Studien Zur Interkulturellen Geschichte Des Christentums, Bd. 116.). Grand Rapids: Peter Lang Publishing, 1999.

Rambo, Lewis R. *Understanding Religious Conversion*. Yale University, 1993.

Randrianasolo, Joseph. *Camp Of Joy Lutheran Church: Where Is Your Child?* Diss., Concordia Theological Seminary, 2009.

_____. "More Reflections Upon Exorcism As A Means Of Grace." E-mail message to author. June 22, 2010.

_____. "Some Reflections About the Dissertation Proposal Written by the Rev. Robert H. Bennett." E-mail message to author. February 14, 2010.

_____. "Spirits in Madagascar." Interview by author. August 3, 2009.

_____. "Spiritual and Traditional Beliefs in the Malagasy Lutheran Church: An Analysis of Fifohazana." 2008. MS, Pretoria, Pretoria.

_____. "The Usefulness of the Lutheran Confessions in the African World." *Dialog: A Journal of Theology* 45, no. 2 (Summer 2006): 127–31.

Ridderbos, Herman. *The Gospel of John: A Theological Commentary.* Boston: Eerdmans, 1997.

Riensche, R. H. "Exegesis of Ephesians 2:1–7." *Lutheran Quarterly* 2, no. 1 (1950): 70–74.

Robinson, John Arthur Thomas. *Redating the New Testament.* New York: Wipf & Stock Publishers, 2000.

Rogers, Alan D. "Human Prudence and Implied Divine Sanctions In Malagasy Proverbial Wisdom." *Journal of Religion in Africa* 15, no. 3 (1985): 216–26.

Rommen, Edward. *Spiritual Power and Missions: Raising the Issues* (Evangelical Missiological Society Series). New York: William Carey Library Publishers, 1995.

Roschke, Ronald W. "Healing in Luke, Madagascar, and Elsewhere." *Currents in Theology and Mission* 33, no. 6 (December 2006): 459–71.

Rosik, Christopher H. "Critical Issues in the Dissociative Disorders Field: Six Perspectives from Religiously Sensitive Practitioners." *Journal of Psychology and Theology* 31, no. 2 (2003): 113–28.

_____. "When Discernment Fails: The Case for Outcome Studies on Exorcism." *Journal of Psychology and Theology* 25, no. 3 (1997): 354–63.

Rupp, E. Gordan, and Philip S. Watson, eds. *Luther and Erasmus: Free Will and Salvation.* Philadelphia: Westminster John Knox Press, 1995.

Ruud, Jørgen. *TABOO: A Study of Malagasy Customs and Beliefs*. Oslo: Oslo University Press, 1960.

_____. *Gods and Ancestors: Society and Religion Among the Forest Tribes in Madagascar*. Oslo: Solum Forlag, Distributed in the U.S.A. by International Specialized Book Services, 2002.

Salib, E., and S. Youakim. "Spiritual Healing in Elderly Psychiatric Patients: A Case-Control Study in an Egyptian Hospital." *Aging & Mental Health* 5, no. 4 (2001): 366–70.

Sargant, William Walters. *Mind Possessed: A Physiology of Possession, Mysticism, and Faith Healing*. Philadelphia: Lippincott, 1974.

Schreiter, Robert J. *Faces of Jesus in Africa*. Maryknoll: Orbis Books, 1991.

Schuetze, Armin W., and Irwin J. Habeck. *The Shepherd under Christ*. Milwaukee: Northwestern, 1974.

Schulz, Klaus Detlev. *Mission from the Cross: the Lutheran Theology of Mission*. St. Louis: Concordia, 2009.

Sharp, Lesley A. *The Possessed and the Dispossessed: Spirits, Identity, and Power in a Madagascar Migrant Town* (Comparative Studies of Health Systems and Medical Care). New York: University of California Press, 1996.

_____. "Wayward Pastoral Ghosts And Regional Xenophobia In A Northern Madagascar Town." *Africa* 71, no. 1 (2001): XX.

Sheppard, Leslie, Lewis Spence, and Nandor Fodor, eds. *Encyclopedia of Occultism & Parapsychology*. 2nd ed. Vol. 2. Detroit: Gale Research, 1984.

Shorter, Aylward. *Jesus and the Witchdoctor: An Approach to Healing and Wholeness*. London: G. Chapman, Orbis Books, 1985.

Singleton, Royce. *Approaches to Social Research*. New York: Oxford University Press, 1999.

Sorensen, Eric. *Possession and Exorcism in the New Testament and Early Christianity*. Tübingen: Mohr Siebeck, 2002.

Spence, Lewis, and Nandor Fodor. *Encyclopedia of Occultism & Parapsychology*. Edited by Leslie Shepard. Vol. 2. Detroit: Gale Research, 1984.

"Spiritual Survey: New Study Points to Rise of Do-It-Yourself Religion." The Wall of Separation. http://blog.au.org/2009/12/10/spiritual-survey-new-study-points-to-rise-of-doityourself-religion/ (accessed February 28, 2010).

Ssettuuma, Benedict. "Mission As Service to Life; Reflections from an African Worldview." *Exchange* 33, no. 2 (2004): 180–98.

Steyne, Philip M. *Gods of Power: A Study of the Beliefs and Practices of Animists*. New York: Impact International Foundation, 1996.

Strong, Augustus Hopkins. *Systematic Theology a Compendium and Commonplace Book Designed for the use of Theological Students*. Philadelphia: Judson Press, 1912.

Summers, Montague. *The History of Witchcraft and Demonology*. Minneapolis: Dover Publications, 2007.

Tappert, Theodore G., ed. *Luther Letters of Spiritual Counsel* (Library of Christian Classics). New York: Westminster John Knox Press, 2006.

_____. *The Book of Concord: The Confessions of the Evangelical Lutheran Church*. New York: Augsburg Fortress, 1959.

Thielicke, Helmut. *I Believe the Christian Creed*. Translated by John W. Doberstein and H. George Anderson. Philadelphia: Fortress Press, 1968.

_____. *Man In God's World*. Translated by John W. Doberstein. New York: Harper & Row, 1963.

_____. *The Evangelical Faith*. Vol. 3. Translated by Geffrey W. Bromiley. 3 vols. Grand Rapids: Eerdmans, 1977.

Thompson, Marianne Meyer. *The Incarnate Word: Perspectives on Jesus in the Fourth Gospel*. New York: Hendrickson Publishers, 1993.

Tillich, Paul. *Systematic Theology: 1: Reason and Revelation Being and God*. Chicago: University of Chicago Press, 1973.

Twelftree, Graham H. *In the Name of Jesus: Exorcism among Early Christians.* Grand Rapids: Baker Academic, 2007.

_____. *Jesus the Exorcist: A Contribution to the Study of the Historical Jesus.* Peabody: Hendrickson, 1993.

Unger, Merrill F. *Demons in the World Today: A Study of Occultism in the Light of God's Word.* New York: Tyndale House, 1973.

Usiwa, Nyakwawa U. "Chipembedzo Cha Makolo Achikuda (African Ancestors' Religion): Intellectualistic and Nationalistic Traits." In *African Ancestors Religion. Chipembedzo cha Makolo Achikuda,* edited by J. C. Chakanza, 62–79. Vol. 21. Hauppauge: Kachere Series, 2006.

Virkler, Henry A., and Mary B. Virkler. "Demonic Involvement in Human Life and Illness." *Journal of Psychology and Theology* 5, no. 2 (1977): 95–103.

Walther, C. F. W. *Walther's Pastorale: That is, American Lutheran Pastoral Theology.* Translated by John M. Dickamer. New Haven: Lutheran News, 1995.

_____. *Proper Distinction Between Law and Gospel.* Translated by W. H. T. Dau. St. Louis: Concordia, 1986.

Warrington, Keith. "Reflections on the History and Development of Demonological Beliefs and Praxis among British Pentecostals." *Asian Journal of Pentecostal Studies,* no. 7, 2nd ser. (2004): 281–304.

Weller, Philip T., trans. *The Roman Ritual: Complete Edition.* Milwaukee: Bruce Publishing, 1964.

Wendland, E. H. *Of Other Gods and Other Spirits.* Milwaukee: Northwestern, 1977.

Wilder, William D. *Journeys of the Soul, Anthropological Studies of Death, Burial and Reburial Practices in Borneo* (Borneo Research Council Monograph Series). Detroit: Borneo Research Council, 2003.

Wimber, John, and Kevin Springer. *Power Evangelism.* London: Holder Christian Paperbacks, 2001.

Wink, Walter. *Naming the Powers the Language of Power in the New Testament.* Philadelphia: Fortress Press, 1984.

Winzeler, Robert L., ed. *Seen and the Unseen: Shamanism, Mediumship and Possession in Borneo*. Williamsburg: Borneo Research Council, 1993.

Witherington, Ben. *John's Wisdom: A Commentary on the Fourth Gospel*. Louisville: Westminster John Knox Press, 1995.

Wright, Christopher J. H. "Implications of Conversion in the Old Testament and the New." *International Bulletin of Missionary Research* 28, no. 1 (2004): 14–19.

Zvomunondita Kurewa, J. N. "Conversion in African Context." *International Review of Mission* 68, no. 270 (1997): 161–66.

SCRIPTURE INDEX

Subject Index

priest(s), priesthood, 4, 57–58,
70, 77, 91, 125, 137–38,
151
protection, 14, 34, 43, 48–49,
52, 54, 59, 88, 133, 169–
70, 172
psychiatric, 153
psychological, 13–14, 55, 150,
156, 160–61
Psychology, 13, 132, 150–51,
156,
purgatory, 151

Rainisoalambo, Dada, 18–19
Rakotozandry, Dadatoa, 19–
20
Randrianandrasana, 21
Randrianasolo, Joseph, 4, 6–7,
11–12, 33–39, 31–42, 44–
47, 52, 96n, 175–76
rationalism, 25, 147, 155, 167,
177
Ratsimanamboina, 36n
Ravelonjanahary, Neny, 19
razana, 38–40, 53, 55–63, 76,
78–82, 89–90, 93, 179–81,
184, 187–88
repentance, 12, 71, 76–79, 81–
82, 149, 182–83
resurrection, 20, 49, 81, 105,
127, 129, 144, 165
revival, 4, 6, 18–19
ridicule, of Satan, 137–38,
142, 146
ritual(s), ritualistic, 16, 20–21,
25, 34, 40–41, 44, 48, 59,

93, 125, 137–39, 190, 46,
102, 132, 146
Roman Rite, 25, 137, 144. *See
also* Roman Ritual
Roman Ritual, 137. *See also*
Roman Rite

Sacrament(s), Sacramental,
87, 92–93, 96, 130, 137,
148, 176
sacrifice(s), sacrificial, 16, 24,
27, 30, 32–34, 55–56, 58–
61, 63, 66, 78, 81, 87
SALT (*Sekoly Ambony
Loterana momba ny
Teolojia*), 7–8, 145, 175
salvation, 87, 96, 124, 130,
140, 148–49, 166, 170
Satan, satanic, 13, 22, 25, 32,
44, 47–48, 52, 54, 77, 82,
90, 99–101, 103–105, 107–
109, 111–115, 117, 119,
121, 123–25, 127–28, 130–
14, 146–49, 151–55, 158–
73
Savior, 31, 46, 47, 144–45,
151
Schulz, Klaus, 12
screaming, 3, 11, 38, 150
secular, 26, 57, 91, 131
sermon(s), 3, 49, 105, 135
serpents, 123, 173
shamanistic, 55,
Sharp, Lesley, 18n, 37–38
Shepherd(s), 7, 17, 19–20, 42,
46, 48–49, 51, 74

sickness(es), 6, 15, 19, 29, 31,
38, 58, 61–63, 66, 73, 77,
81–82, 108, 113–14, 135–
36
sikidy, 61
slavery, 82–83, 157
snake(s), 38, 173
Soatanana, 15–19, 21, 23, 25,
27, 29, 31
Solomon, 99–100
spiritual(ism), 22, 25–28, 30–
32, 25–27, 29, 41–42, 44,
54–58, 60, 62, 65–66, 70–
72, 76–77, 86–87, 89–91,
103, 127, 135–36, 139,
146, 148–151, 153, 155–
59, 164, 172–74, 176–80
strength, 23, 47, 96, 150, 170
struggle(s), 66, 70, 76–78,
140–141, 173, 176
suffered, suffering(s), 18, 54,
56, 67, 77, 81, 117, 138,
153–54
suicide, 139–140
superhuman, 150
supernatural, 125, 150
superstition(s), superstitious,
83, 127n, 153, 157
syncretism, 6, 32, 43, 57, 87–
88, 92, 96, 126, 177, 184

taboo(s), 55, 59, 76, 80–83,
89–90, 92
talisman, 58, 61, 68–69
telepathy, 150n
temptation(s), 93, 132–34, 141

terror, 80, 82, 143
Thielicke, Helmut, 156–60,
167
threatened, 65, 67, 159
toby, 18–22, 26–27, 42, 48n,
51, 64, 69, 73–75, 94–95,
178
Toliara, 3, 48
tomb(s), 24, 36–41, 59–60, 93,
165
tromba, 23, 37–38, 43, 43, 56,
58, 62, 66–67, 70, 73, 76–
77, 80–82

unconscious, 44, 67, 73

vazimba, 36–37
vestments, 20
Visitation, 172–174

Walther, C. F. W., 148–54,
166–67
Wimber, John, 9–12
witchcraft, 161
worldview(s), 5, 7–8, 11, 15–
16, 21, 25–27, 31–32, 34–
35, 42, 53–54, 56, 62, 66
worship(ed), 3, 20–21, 23, 36,
22, 24, 28, 33–34, 36–37,
42–43, 46, 54, 61, 63, 69,
71, 79, 81, 87–88, 90, 96,
131, 169–71

Zanahary, 35–36
zavarindrano, 63. *See also*
ambirorandrano; mermaid

Peer Reviewed

Concordia Publishing House

Similar to the peer review or "refereed" process used to publish professional and academic journals, the Peer Review process is designed to enable authors to publish book manuscripts through Concordia Publishing House. The Peer Review process is well-suited for smaller projects and textbook publication.

We aim to provide quality resources for congregations, church workers, seminaries, universities, and colleges. Our books are faithful to the Holy Scriptures and the Lutheran Confessions, promoting the rich theological heritage of the historic, creedal Church. Concordia Publishing House (CPH) is the publishing arm of The Lutheran Church—Missouri Synod. We develop, produce, and distribute (1) resources that support pastoral and congregational ministry, and (2) scholarly and professional books in exegetical, historical, dogmatic, and practical theology.

**For more information, visit:
www.cph.org/PeerReview.**